Wrong Time, Wrong Place?

Wrong Time, Wrong Place?

How Two Canadians Ended Up in a Brazilian Jail

CAROLINE MALLAN

KEY PORTER BOOKS

Canadian Cataloguing in Publication Data

Mallan, Caroline
Wrong time, wrong place? : how two Canadians ended up in a Brazilian prison

Includes index
ISBN 1-55013-623-2

1. Lamont, Christine. 2. Spencer, David.
3. Diniz, Abilio dos Santos – Kidnapping, 1989.
4. Kidnapping – Brazil. 5. Canadian – Brazil.
I. Title.

HV6604.B732D55 1995 364.1'54'0922 C94-932859-6

The publisher gratefully acknowledges the assistance of the Canada Council, the Department of Communications, and the Government of Ontario.

Key Porter Books Limited
70 The Esplanade
Toronto, Ontario
Canada M5E 1R2

Design: Jean Lightfoot Peters
Typesetting: MacTrix DTP
Printed and bound in Canada

95 96 97 98 99 6 5 4 3 2 1

Contents

To my parents,
Liam and Anne Mallan

Acknowledgements

I relied on countless people for information and help in piecing together Christine and David's story. The most difficult to thank are the many who asked to remain nameless: the friends of Christine and David who love the jailed couple but could no longer witness in silence the campaign to free them and the toll it was taking; the supporters who felt that enough was enough; police investigators in Canada, the United States, Brazil, and Europe; diplomats who knew the case; and politicians who were surprisingly forthcoming.

At the *Toronto Star*, I would like to thank Dave Ellis, Greg Smith, and Steve Tustin. A special thanks to Don Sellar for his tidbits, and to Peter Edwards and Kellie Hudson for their encouragement and advice. At Key Porter, thanks to Jonathan Webb. Thank you to my family and to Colin for their unwavering support and patience.

PROLOGUE

RALLY FOR JUSTICE

JOIN MARILYN LAMONT
ON PARLIAMENT HILL
Thursday, February 11, 1993
2:00 PM
As she leads a demonstration to free
her daughter Christine and fiancee [*sic*] David Spencer
They have been wrongly accused!!!

THE MULRONEY GOVERNMENT
has seen fit to keep
two young Canadians in Brazil
prisons for
THREE FULL YEARS.

The Justice Committee of the House of Commons says
there was
"A MISCARRIAGE OF JUSTICE"
Everyday in Brazilian prisons is a
THREAT TO THEIR SAFETY AND THEIR HEALTH

THE POSTERS WERE EVERYWHERE IN OTTAWA DURING THE FEW DAYS preceding the planned rally on the Hill. United Church congregations in the Ottawa area were asked to include the leaflets advertising the rally in their bulletins. The leaflets were also stuck on lampposts and hoardings and pinned to bulletin boards at the city's universities. It was important to bring out as many supporters as possible. The number of people who joined the rally would mean a great deal. The government had to get the message that thousands of Canadians were calling for the release of the imprisoned Canadians.

Marilyn Lamont, a petite silvery-blonde woman in her early sixties, was scheduled to fly in for the rally from her home in Langley, British Columbia. Her visit would be brief, part of a series of events that was to include a similar rally in Toronto, and a meeting with reporters at the Royal York Hotel.

In every rally, in every city she visited, the theme was always the same: Her daughter had been wrongly convicted for taking part in a brutal kidnapping in Brazil. Christine was innocent. And yet, despite her youth and innocence, she was serving a twenty-eight-year sentence in a Brazilian jail. Worst of all, the Canadian government refused to help bring her home.

Marilyn's husband, Keith, would not be able to join her on this trip. Although he was approaching retirement age, Keith Lamont, a tall, lanky former university basketball player, was showing no sign of slowing down. It was Keith's work as a surgeon at Langley Memorial Hospital that paid for his wife's trips across Canada, for the couple's regular visits to Brazil, for their lawyers — for all the expenses involved in their battle to rescue Christine. Without the support of the couple's many friends in the tightly-knit British Columbia community, they might not have been able to keep up the struggle for as long as they had.

The day of the Ottawa rally dawned bitterly cold and grey. It was not the sort of weather that drew protestors in droves. In fact, only fifteen people braved the biting wind to stand alongside Marilyn as she waved a placard bearing the words "Justice Now — Lamont and Spencer."

Small as it was, the group took up a chant addressed to the federal government: "Bring them home!" And then Marilyn spoke. She began by complaining about the woman who was then the Minister for External Affairs.

"Barbara McDougall is willing to let Christine and David sit and rot rather than ask for their expulsion [from Brazil]," she said, her voice barely carrying in the wind.

As Marilyn spoke, she was joined on the steps of Parliament Hill by five members of the House of Commons Justice Committee, including its chairman, Progressive Conservative MP Bob Horner, who endorsed the family's request to have the External Affairs Minister ask that Brazil send the two jailed Canadians home.

The protestors, almost all of whom were human-rights activists from a local congregation of the United Church, then took up the chant again. They were led by a passionate young man who wore a business suit that did little to keep out the cold, his hand-made sign rattling in the icy wind. The others in the small circle of protestors guessed that he was an old friend of either Christine or David. In fact, he was a paid employee of an influential Ottawa lobbyist, paid to be there, paid to lead the protestors.

The demonstration, small as it was, did not go unnoticed. *The Ottawa Citizen* described it in a short piece the next morning. It may not have been the success that Marilyn had hoped for, but it would still be worth it if it had caught the attention of a few more people, people willing to help her in her fight to free her daughter. Action was needed — before it was too late.

Only a few months earlier, police in São Paulo had quelled deadly riots that claimed the lives of more than 100 inmates at prisons adjacent to the one occupied by the Canadian couple. The possibility of sudden violence, the risk of disease, and Christine's failing health were all sources of anguish and worry on the part of her parents.

Marilyn and Keith Lamont could not understand their government's refusal to help. Christine and David's case was so clearly an injustice. They were young. They were idealistic. They had set out to help the people of Latin America but found themselves in over their heads with a gang of international terrorists, people capable of heinous crimes. It was these others, these terrorists, who had used David and Christine. It was the terrorists who had tricked them into seeming to participate in the kidnapping of a Brazilian multi-millionaire. When David and Christine were arrested for the kidnapping along with the others, the seasoned revolutionaries, they were simply in the wrong place at the wrong time. God help them — their own government wouldn't.

PART I:
CHRISTINE AND DAVID

CHAPTER 1

AN EXPERIMENTAL UNIVERSITY

CHRISTINE LAMONT'S FIRST FORAY INTO POST-SECONDARY EDUCATION was not a success. In 1977, after graduating from high school in Surrey, B.C., she enrolled in an arts program at the University of British Columbia in Vancouver. School friends remember that she wanted to get out of her parents' house, to move from surburban Langley to downtown Vancouver, with its famed West Coast atmosphere and droves of young people looking for answers about what to do with the rest of their lives. But, like thousands of others coming to a big university from a small town, Christine found the large campus disorienting and the array of courses overwhelming. She dropped out before the end of her first year.

It is not clear whether Christine lacked the concentration required for university studies or was unwilling to make the commitment to a career path at this stage of her life. At UBC, students were required to specialize, choosing their major field of interest, in second year. Hard decisions had to be made, and perhaps Christine was not ready to make them. A woman who became her friend a few years later, Mary Sibierski, said Christine had told her that she didn't think university had anything to teach her at that point.

Having given up on university studies for the time being, Christine bounced through a variety of minimum-wage jobs, including work at a cookie company and as a salesclerk at the Pacific National Exhibition, before landing a position with an import/export company that dealt primarily with merchandise from Southeast Asia. Christine began there as a clerk, but, as her time with the company accumulated, her responsibilities grew, and she earned the trust of her employers, to the point that they once sent her to assist on a jewellery-buying trip to Thailand. But the small company was hard-hit by the recession that swept through Canada in 1982, and Christine was again unemployed when the company declared bankruptcy.

More time slipped away from her, and by her mid-twenties Christine still had not formulated a game plan for where she was going and what she was going to do. Whereas this lack of direction had mattered less when she was younger, as the record-breaking boom of the mid-1980s replaced the recession, Christine was at a point in her life when her peers were finished their schooling and well on their way to successful careers. Some of them, at least, were taking advantage of the sudden turnaround in the economy that had brought about a level of prosperity in Canada that will be remembered for decades to come. The mid-1980s meant there was a good job opportunity awaiting virtually every university graduate with the will to work. Christine's friends had seized that opportunity and were getting married, having children, and buying houses, while Christine was back working at odd jobs, living off and on in her parents' house, and relying on a steady income from a family company known as Lamont Holdings. As Christine continued to search for direction in her life, money wasn't an issue. Her family supported her and offered their help at every turn.

Christine enrolled as a mature student in the Communications department at Simon Fraser University in September 1985 — almost thirty years to the day after the "experimental" university had opened. Gordon Shrum, the former chairman of B.C. Hydro, the huge public utility, called it that when he took on the job of chancellor, building a second university in British Columbia's lower mainland. One of Shrum's objectives was to ensure that SFU did not mirror the University of British Columbia, with its massive, spread-out campus and impersonal atmosphere. Rather, SFU would be an intimate school on a compact campus, high up a winding, tree-lined road on Burnaby Mountain, isolated and distinctive, both in its physical structure and in its teaching philosophy.

Shrum, describing his work at SFU for a biographer, said: "I wanted an experimental university where no hard and fast rules inhibited faculty from modifying courses, pursuing interdisciplinary studies, or developing creative new programs. I wanted SFU to be a place where new ideas would flourish and creative people would flock in."

As the years passed and Simon Fraser emerged as one of the most controversial and radical universities in North America, Shrum's wish would come true. Academics from around the world came to lend their talents to the school. It quickly developed a national reputation for left-wing politics that went beyond the activism seen on other campuses across Canada in the 1960s.

SFU was one of the first campuses to witness the massive student protests and demonstrations against the Vietnam War. In November 1968, students occupied the university's administration building to protest what they called "discriminatory admissions practices." The RCMP were given access to students' files while students themselves were denied such access. At one point the university called in 200 RCMP officers to remove 114 students from the building.

This alternative spirit, of a generation that dared to question the beliefs and politics of their parents and the leadership of their nation, lives on at Simon Fraser. Students today hark back to the days of meaningful protest, and the university's reputation still projects an aura of radicalism. It was into this setting, where inquiry and critical debate had flourished for years, that Christine Lamont wandered in 1985, still unsure of exactly what it was she was there to discover or learn.

It seems that it did not take Christine long to find her footing at the university that Gordon Shrum built. By the start of her second year at SFU, she had taken an introductory course in Latin American history. This class would provide Christine with the spark and the passion for this beleaguered part of the world that would cause her to switch her major to Latin American Studies, a respected program of courses offered by several departments, including history, politics, and literature. Christine's elective introductory course was taught by Professor Ronald Newton. Intended for novice students of history and politics, it was in many respects an overview of the history of the region, a history consisting of horror stories about small nations overrun and exploited by European adventurers and home-grown tyrants, a history of oppression and resistance, revolution and rule enforced by sword and gun.

The history studied in Professor Newton's course was combined with frequent updates on what was happening in Latin America's trouble spots at that time. El Salvador, in particular, was a regular topic of conversation as tales of that small nation's misery under the governance of an American-backed president reached students by way of the refugees who had escaped through the United States and made their way north.

Civil war had raged in El Salvador since October 1979, when a military coup overthrew the government of General Carlos Humberto Romero, and the left-wing rebel insurgency began in earnest. The rebel group was the product of a coalition of five different movements that were united under the banner of the Farabundo Martí National Liberation Front (FMLN), named after Augustin

Farabundo Martí, who had led a 1932 Communist uprising. Martí's revolt resulted in the slaughter of thirty thousand peasants by the military in what is still remembered in El Salvador as "La Matanza"—the massacre. The trademark of the modern Salvadorean civil war was the notorious death squads that captured, tortured, and killed anyone who dared to question the military's rule. The arbitrary targeting of civilians for death by the military subsided marginally after the May 1984 electoral win of José Napoleón Duarte's centrist Christian Democrats, who, with the support of the United States, captured 54 per cent of the vote. But the guerrilla war waged by the FMLN continued from the hills of Salvador, paralysing local governments and making commerce all but impossible. The estimated seven thousand FMLN insurgents ordered travel bans, blew up power and telecommunications stations, and set land mines that crippled the plantation-style agriculture of the tiny nation. El Salvador relied on aid from the United States to keep it from collapsing into financial ruin and the United States obliged, pumping an estimated $2 million a day into El Salvador in the hopes of keeping the Marxist-influenced FMLN at bay. The fighting consumed 40 per cent of the national budget. But, in 1986, seven years after the onset of the civil war, the situation remained stalemated. Salvadorean guerrillas imported arms from neighbouring Nicaragua, where the socialist Sandinista government was sympathetic to their cause, but there was a limit to what Nicaragua could spare. To continue the struggle the guerrillas needed to drum up support outside of Latin America. They needed donations, arms, and supplies, and they were running out of time. Even those sympathetic to their cause in Salvador were tiring of the toll the war had taken, with an estimated sixty thousand people, mainly civilians, dead as a direct result of the conflict. A willingness to compromise was beginning to emerge. Many people in Salvador were demanding an end to the war, even if it meant accepting the rule of Duarte's government. Rumours were circulating to the effect that some of the most active death squads from the early 1980s had re-formed, and a new wave of killings could be expected. For the people who had been unable to flee Salvador, the prospect was too awful: they were losing the will to fight. Sacrifice in the name of socialism could no longer be stoically endured.

Daily news reports detailing the suffering in Salvador, along with the perspective gained from Professor Newton's class, affected Christine as nothing had before. Although the course was worth only a half-credit, for Christine it was an inspiration, firing her with an enthusiasm to do more, to become involved—to help.

Christine's switch from her communications major to political science at the start of her second year coincided with a growth in the number of on-campus activities with which she was involved. Despite her love of her newfound subject, Christine's activism outside the classroom was taking away from the time she had to devote to her studies. Professors and teaching assistants remember her as one of those students who drift in and out of courses, without ever seeming totally committed to the more laborious aspects of course work, such as research papers. But she was always very interested in discussions with her classmates and the opinions of her professors. At about the time she was becoming engrossed in the issue of political tyranny, Christine started to dress unconventionally. Now that she was free of the workaday world and of the dress code that going to work and dealing with customers demanded, Christine began to follow the trends set by Britain's punk rock movement. She wore black from head to toe, and flowing outfits with long skirts that trailed on the floor behind her. Her fair complexion was made paler by white make-up, and heavy black eyeliner gave her face a haunted look. The dozens of tiny silver rings on her fingers and the multiple silver hoop earrings she wore were handcrafted and Asian in style, showing the influence of the import/export company she had worked for. It was through her courses in Latin American Studies and involvement in campus activities that Christine met Keith Hughes. Hughes shared Christine's interest in El Salvador and her concerns about the restrictions on speech and personal freedom there.

The more they learned, the more outraged they became, and their desire to help grew to the point where books, classes, and lectures were not enough.

It is here that the Christine Lamonts and Keith Hugheses of this world entered the struggle that belonged to the people of El Salvador.

CHAPTER 2

RADIO DAYS

DAVID SPENCER WAS THE BABY OF THE FAMILY, THE ONLY BOY AND the little brother to two sisters. Both his sisters, Bev, fourteen years older than David, and Judith, seven years his senior, had attended university, making their parents proud. At age eighteen, after he graduated from Harrison Trimble High School on Echo Drive in Moncton, New Brunswick, in 1981, David, too, enrolled at Mount Allison University in nearby Sackville. He chose a liberal arts course of study that included psychology, sociology, biology, English, and economics. In the third week of September 1981, one week after classes had begun, David telephoned his father, Bill, and told him he didn't think university was for him and he wanted to quit. Bill Spencer asked him if he had even bought his books yet, and when David admitted he hadn't, he suggested that David have a good look at the course material before making any rash decisions. David said that he was pretty certain it wouldn't work out and didn't want to waste his parents' hard-earned money, but his father replied that he had worked hard for that money so that his children could have the things he'd never had — specifically, an education.

The telephone conversation ended with father and son agreeing that David would give it another crack and buy the books.

That weekend, David went to the Moncton apartment of his girlfriend, Sue Cormier. He had met her during his last year of high school when she worked at a local record store where David had spent a lot of time, checking out the latest music to find its way to New Brunswick. David spent the weekend complaining to Sue that he hated the university, the people, the restrictive atmosphere, and was determined to quit. Sue felt that she couldn't change his mind, that a small-town university, full of conservative, like-minded people from the Maritimes' upper crust, was not the ideal place for a young man like David. Sue remembers that David was changing fast, and the direction his life was taking seemed to be on a collision course with everything Mount Allison represented. Two more weeks passed before David again phoned his father. This time he seemed adamant and insisted that no more money be wasted on keeping him somewhere that he didn't want to be. David said he was coming home. Bill Spencer was disappointed, but gave his son credit for owning up to not belonging, which was braver than sitting in Sackville, doing nothing and hating every minute of it.

Bill and his wife, Jean, were there at the door a few days later to welcome David back to their modest bungalow in northwest Moncton. The house was on a quiet street, just down the road from David's junior school. It was the same street where David had played ball hockey on the road with the neighbours' kids and dreamed of becoming a goalie in the National Hockey League. He had been a big fan of the Montreal Canadiens' great goaltender Ken Dryden, and had never failed to watch him on "Hockey Night in Canada."

Bill Spencer had grown up in the working-class town of Saint John, New Brunswick, an industrial port city. The Great Depression had robbed him of the education that he later so desperately desired for his own family. In 1930, when he was just twelve, his parents were evicted from their tenement housing and were forced to rent rooms in a large building that doubled as a local brothel, frequented by sailors from the docks. By the time Bill was fourteen, his father was dead, and the boy quit school and went to work to help support his family. He is a man who knows what poverty is all about, and he has lived in hope that his three children would never acquire the same hard knowledge. Bill served his country in the Canadian army during the Second World War as an army cook. After the war, he took a position as a cooking teacher at the Moncton campus of New Brunswick Community College.

By this time, Bill had met and married Jean, who shared his working-class background and desire to provide something more for their young family. Jean had grown up in Toronto's Parkdale neighbourhood, which in her time was a respectable community housing mainly factory workers, people who put in an honest day's work for their paycheque. The area that Bill and Jean Spencer remembered so fondly from summer visits with their kids has since become the precinct of drug addicts, pushers, and prostitutes, making it one of that city's least desirable places to live and most dangerous neighbourhoods after dark.

Various reasons have been suggested for David's decision to leave school. Friends of his parents say the boy just wasn't ready for serious study. He had always been a shy, quiet young man and had not found his voice until the year before enrolling so hadn't grown up enough. The last thing he seemed interested in was being shipped off to an even smaller town to go to school.

But those who knew David Spencer well during his final year at Harrison Trimble say that four years at a small-town university was not in the plans of a young man who had developed a strong sense of social justice, along with a measure of sophistication that distanced him from his peers. David had developed a liking for punk music. Because of his friendship with Sue Cormier, and Marc

Gaudet, who worked alongside Sue at the record store, David became a regular fixture at the Sam the Record Man store in Champlain Mall, near the community of Dieppe on the outskirts of Moncton. It was here that he was introduced to the likes of The Ramones, The Sex Pistols, and The Clash, a sharp contrast to the techno-pop sound left over from years of disco. As David entered his final year at Harrison Trimble, where he had neither many friends nor remarkable grades, he went beyond just listening to punk music and began to dress the part. In a conservative town like Moncton, the sudden appearance of David in black jeans and a leather jacket, and with his head shaved, drew more than a couple of passing glances. People in the streets stared at the "weirdo." At school, David ran the risk of a run-in with the "hard-core AC/DC guys," as one classmate described the "headbangers" of the school community, youths who didn't look favourably on the promotion of any kind of music unlike their preferred heavy metal. They would gladly beat up anyone who dared to be different or who implied that there was something wrong with their music. For a skinny, short (about five feet, nine inches) kid like David, punk gear could have easily spelled trouble. But acquaintances say he seemed to be able to handle himself. He stayed calm and walked away from potential confrontations, never bothering to incite his adversaries.

David provided the screaming vocals for The Robins, a local punk band made up of four or five buddies, and spent an increasing amount of time in friends' basements and garages, rehearsing new songs and smoking pot.

Teachers who had had David as a student in Grades 10 and 11 had to look up his picture to jog their memory about the thin boy who wore glasses, but those who taught him during his punk phase remember the bizarre outfits and the shaved head of an otherwise very average student who neither excelled nor failed in his schoolwork. David did not participate in a single organized sport in high school and, while he later said he worked on the school newspaper, no one from his time at Harrison Trimble remembers his contribution. Similarly, no one in Moncton remembers him playing little league baseball or hockey, or belonging to Boy Scouts or any other community group. The transformation from obscure nobody to attention-seeking punker was remarkable and speedy. For the person David had become in such a short time, Mount Allison would have been an odd setting. The new David, with eccentric tastes and monochrome leather wardrobe, was never meant to spend his youth in Sackville.

David spent most of the fall of 1981 in Moncton hanging out with his friends, listening to the latest imported records from Britain, and trying to get gigs for his struggling band. After New Year's 1982, he and Sue Cormier decided to try life elsewhere and packed up. They travelled first to Toronto, then Winnipeg where they both found jobs and stayed for a while. But just over a year later, David was back living in Moncton, in a small apartment on Wesley Street in the downtown area. He started a cheaply produced, newsprint fanzine which offered news about the world of alternative music to its most ardent fans. As an independent publisher, no matter on how small a scale, David frequently had access to free passes for concerts in East Coast venues, including Halifax. As well, he managed to submerge himself completely in the local band scene once again.

In a place like Moncton, things change very slowly. David's buddies from his high school days were still busy with local bands, still living with their parents, still smoking up in the garage most nights of the week and dreaming of life in the big time. Marc Gaudet, one of David's closest friends in Moncton, had tried to make a go of it in Toronto for a couple of years but had returned home to his family and his job at the record store in the mall. He had, by the time David returned, gone through two or three new bands, and he and David picked up where they had left off a couple of years earlier.

However, Moncton still didn't have what it took to hold David and, within a matter of months, with only two or three issues of his fanzine behind him, he was heading west again. This time he joined Sue in Vancouver, a city with a long history of taking in people from everywhere else, be they Canadians, American draft dodgers from the Vietnam War, or Chinese immigrants whose ancestors had come for the back-breaking work of building Canada's national railway. It's a city that many say offers a new perspective on life and a beautiful, mountainous backdrop for it. It was this city that David would come to think of as home. In Sue's words, the pair were "into punk music and rebellion" and couldn't find much of either in Moncton. Sue said the first time she and David saw a peace march through the streets of downtown Vancouver, they were in awe. Such a thing is unheard of in Moncton, even to this day. For David, it symbolized all that was right about Vancouver, and all that was wrong with his home town.

David and Sue had come a long way from home together. They had passed into adulthood together and cared for each other. But, by 1983, it was as though they had come to a crossroads in their lives, and the distractions and appeals of this new, vibrant city drew them out and away from each other. It was at this interchange that their paths diverged: they split as a couple, remaining friends but realizing that a good shared history was no guarantee of a solid shared future.

David's life in Vancouver was not glamorous. He worked washing dishes, busing tables, doing odd jobs to earn some money. His love of punk music drew him to after-hours clubs to hear struggling new bands. He had a strong desire to get involved with like-minded people, people who weren't happy with the status quo in Canada, people who were looking for something more radical that might provide more answers. David's yearnings for company drew him to Vancouver's alternative radio station and a cast of characters who offered a chance for David to meet all sorts of people affiliated with a variety of groups, among them the International Socialists, women's rights advocates, and peace activists.

David soon befriended the movers in Vancouver's punk community. One of the players on the scene during David's early days in Vancouver was a guy named Gerry Useless, who played with a band known as The Subhumans, known for songs such as "Burn It Down" and "Slave to My Dick." Gerry Useless would grab headlines across the country in 1983 when he was arrested and accused of being a member of a group that came to be known as the Squamish Five.

A daring morning arrest on a foggy, rain-swept, winding highway leading out of Vancouver to the ruggedly scenic scapes of famed Whistler had made national headlines. It was January 20, 1983, and the RCMP had just closed the net on the first terrorists to strike Canada since the FLQ-orchestrated October Crisis in 1970. The members of Direct Action, the group responsible for a massive explosion at the Litton Systems plant in Etobicoke, a Toronto suburb, and several other terrorist acts, had been captured. They were renamed the Squamish Five by the media, after the scenic highway where they had been stopped as they drove to target practice in the secluded woods north of the village of Squamish, pulled from their pickup truck, and forced to the wet tarmac and handcuffed.

The gang of five had been on the lam for more than three months, and under heavy RCMP surveillance for much of that time. Ten people in Toronto were still recovering from injuries received in the $3.8-million explosion, and police were also investigating the group in connection with an explosion at the Cheekey-Dunsmuir hydro substation on Vancouver Island and the November 22, 1982, fire-bombings of three Vancouver Red Hot Video outlets, which sold pornography.

Direct Action seemed to be a terrorist organization that suited the needs of anyone with an axe to grind. If you were worried about the pristine forests of Vancouver Island, you could bomb substations with the group; if opposition to nuclear war was your cause, you could blow sky high the company that designed the guidance system for the U.S.–built cruise missile, capable of delivering nuclear warheads with chilling accuracy. If radical feminism that denounced pornography was your passion, then it didn't take much to make a gasoline bomb and level retailers that trafficked in it. Despite their talent for destruction, Direct Action was essentially a club for young anarchists who did not want to be accountable to anyone. For them, moral righteousness ruled the day and made them unanswerable for their actions. They conspired to rob a Brinks truck outside a Woolco store at the Lougheed Mall in Burnaby, not far from Simon Fraser University. After all, there wasn't much money in the life of a modern-day anarchist and, as convicted terrorist Juliet Belmas would later explain, "It takes so much energy and mental energy and sweat, you couldn't hold a full-time job [while being a terrorist]."

During the RCMP hunt for the culprits, the Squamish Five stoked Canadians' passion and fear about the resurfacing of terrorism on this land, which had managed to regain much of its innocence after the FLQ crisis. The gang was despised by the Canadian public, by the people who relax in the comfort of knowing that the kind of terrorist struggles that beset Northern Ireland with the Irish Republican Army and Italy with the Red Brigades will never touch them directly at home. When the take-down happened on that lonely B.C. highway, the Squamish Five did not rush to the forefront of public sympathy, but in the underworld of anarchists and radicals, congratulations were handed out and notes of support issued for the Litton bombing. For the terrorists, the majority opinion of mainstream society that found their actions repugnant had long since been deemed irrelevant and corrupt.

David Spencer was fairly new to Vancouver when the trials of the Squamish Five took place in suburban New Westminster, B.C., in late 1983 and early 1984. Through his punk friends in Vancouver, he was able to join a support group of fellow radicals that had sprung up and hastily crafted placards to wave outside the courthouse, in protest over the amount of intense media scrutiny bearing down on the proceedings. David Spencer's tie to the Squamish Five before their arrest is a tenuous one. It is unlikely that he had ever encountered Brent Taylor, the intellectual leader of the group and the man who drove the van in which the 250-kilogram dynamite bomb was hidden, up to the spot outside the wall of Litton Systems where he thought it would do the most damage. Nor is it likely that David had met Ann Hansen, the feminist who fought both pornography and the nuclear arms race as part of the "Wimmin's Fire Brigade," or Doug Stewart, the peace activist/explosives expert who wanted to preserve the natural habitat of Vancouver Island fervently enough to cause $3.7 million in damage to the hydro substation. But whether or not David Spencer's path ever crossed that of a man named Gerry Hannah, also known as Gerry Useless of The Subhumans, is unclear. Hannah, and his girlfriend, Juliet Belmas, described by the prosecution as the foot-soldiers for Direct Action on its missions in Toronto and Vancouver, were part of Vancouver's punk community, as David was. Hannah had often played benefit concerts for peace groups and the anti-nuclear movement; David had been involved with both and had even helped organize some fund-raisers for them. Even if Gerry and David had never met face to face, they moved in the same circles and shared the same friends, hang-outs, tastes, and politics.

What they had in common may be one of the reasons David had for making his way from his shabby apartment on Salsbury Drive in East Vancouver to New Westminster's courthouse to voice his opposition to the treatment given the Squamish Five by the national press gathered outside the courthouse, boom microphones hanging overhead, tape recorders ready for a clip from the lawyers at the end of each day. The protesters called the coverage sensational and blown out of proportion. The portrayal of the gang as cold-hearted criminals, dangerously warped would-be murderers, was false, the protesters said. After all, a warning had been called in to Litton Systems. The fact that it had been delivered too late to spare the workers racing to evacuate the sprawling high-technology complex serious injury was not mentioned, but the protesters pointed out again and again that no one had been killed, as if that explained away the destruction, the maiming of the individuals involved, and the shattering of the innocence of a nation that had for so long been free of the fear of terrorist bombs.

Christine Lamont's friend, Keith Hughes, also found a way to combine his desire for meaningful activism with his other passion — punk music. He had begun working as a volunteer with Vancouver's Co-op Radio. Co-op, a non-profit community radio station, operated out of the third floor of a dingy tower at the corner of Carrall and Hastings streets in Vancouver's historic, cobblestoned Gastown district. The station had none of the modern conveniences of commercial radio and scraped by on donations and limited government funding. Inside, an array of outdated and broken office furniture was scattered among the old couches that have served as beds for a good many volunteers over the years. The Hastings area of Vancouver is rough, with lots of small, smoky taverns selling cheap draft beer by the glass. The alcove leading into the dark stairway that takes visitors up to the heart of the station reeks of urine. At the top of the stairs there is an electronically controlled security door to protect those working inside. For all its crudeness, the station drew droves of volunteers, mainly young people who were eager to learn something about radio and possibly make a difference on the political scene at the same time.

It was in these creaky surroundings that Keith Hughes began co-hosting and co-producing an off-the-cuff radio program that featured the latest and loudest music on the punk scene, interspersed with zany skits poking fun at British Columbia's Social Credit government's policies and at the mainstream media. The show was called "85 RPM" and featured interviews with Vancouver-area activists who were recorded between sets of eardrum-piercing music. It was through this work that Keith Hughes developed lasting ties with Vancouver's refugee community and formed a lasting friendship with his co-host on "85 RPM" — David Spencer.

It was during the fall semester, 1986, that Christine Lamont also became involved with Co-op Radio. She signed up, along with five other SFU students, to help produce a show called "El Salvador Today." The show included interviews with refugees but was mainly a news source, updating its audience on the latest developments in Salvador, mainly from an FMLN perspective. The program reported on their battles and victories, carried stories from their strongholds, and usually ended with a plea for help and support for the tiny war-torn nation of almost five million people.

"El Salvador Today" was broadcast every Wednesday afternoon. The bulk of the show came to Vancouver listeners via a sister station in Managua, Nicaragua. The information about the activities of the rebels was fed to the Managua station by ham-radio operators working clandestinely out of San Salvador and FMLN strongholds around the Salvadorean countryside. These reports were then translated in Managua and relayed to community radio stations across Canada and the United States. In Ontario, the community radio station in Windsor was among the first to bring the program to that province. It was soon followed by Toronto stations based at the University of Toronto and Ryerson Polytechnical Institute (now called Ryerson Polytechnic University).

Co-op Radio Vancouver aired its first instalment of "El Salvador Today" on November 5, 1986, and the Simon Fraser student newspaper, *The Peak*, wrote a story about the six students who were involved in the project. Christine Lamont was the only one quoted in the story, and she described her motivations in deciding to get involved and told the paper's reporter that she hoped the program would bring listeners valuable information that was missing in the mainstream Canadian press. As an example, Christine spoke of the relief efforts that had been mounted after Salvador was shaken by a deadly quake the previous month. Some 250,000 people were left homeless as a result of the disaster, and they were known in the country as the *damnificados*, the damned. Christine pointed out that aid money sent by foreign governments wasn't reaching them.

"The aid isn't going to the people who need it," Christine said. She added that aid sent to El Salvador was, in fact, being channelled into refurbishing the U.S.–backed military, not to providing shelter and fresh drinking water for the *damnificados*. On campus, Christine increased the time she spent organizing protests and rallies in support of the repressed and impoverished people of El Salvador. It was an exciting time on campus: the politics of Latin America were changing rapidly, and student awareness was on the rise, lending an air of shared purpose and a sense of real progress to the people at the heart of the student movement.

Christine had been in the peace business more than a year when, in early 1987, she and Keith Hughes joined a delegation of Canadian students planning a trip to El Salvador as guests of the students' union at the Universidad Nacional de El Salvador, which had seen many of its members killed by the much-feared extreme-right Treasury Police. Foreigners were being invited by fellow students for two reasons: first, to show them firsthand what it was they were helping to fight for, and, second, to gain from the presence of foreigners from nations with near-flawless human-rights records a dose of security. It was thought that the feared Treasury Police, who were suspected of providing the personnel for the death squads that had decimated the university community, would think twice before shooting if they knew they might have to answer to a foreign government, especially one that was providing them with aid.

The march for peace that was the main objective of the trip was to mark the anniversary of the murder of Roman Catholic archbishop Oscar Arnulfo Romero, shot dead in 1980 while serving mass. Of the more than three thousand people who were brave enough to turn out for the march, about two hundred students from the university's delegation shoved past astonished and fuming Treasury Police and scrawled "Yankee invader" and other slogans on the walls of the U.S. embassy. It was a tactic that astonished the Salvadoreans, who were not used to such brazen acts.

Christine Lamont and Keith Hughes formed the Simon Fraser delegation. It was the first trip to Central America for both of them. Christine's parents, Keith and Marilyn Lamont, reluctantly helped finance the ten-day trip after receiving many reassurances from their daughter that she would be safe. The Lamonts, despite being worried about her safety, saw it as a great opportunity for Christine, and friends of the family say that her parents were pleased that Christine seemed to be taking a real and lasting interest in something for the first time in years.

Christine and Keith Hughes had come to know dozens of people in the Vancouver refugee community, who had told them their harrowing stories of murder, torture, and intimidation, but actually going to El Salvador to see for themselves what was happening turned out to be a revelation for both of them. The trip gave Christine a new perspective on the idea of student life. She and Keith came face to face with the military police during the march near the end of their visit, and the bravery and conviction of their Salvadorean colleagues impressed both of them, and helped them realize that taking part in the odd demonstration on a Canadian campus simply wasn't enough to make a real difference. Christine returned home vowing to do more, to take a more active role, to follow the lesson of her Salvadorean colleagues and take more of a risk for what she believed in.

Mary Sibierski, who knew Christine well in her first year at Simon Fraser, said that trip seemed to signal a new beginning for

Christine. "She came back different, really into it. We were going in different directions at that point, but I noticed the difference," remembers Sibierski.

Christine and Keith returned to Canada mid-way through the winter semester at Simon Fraser. Christine threw herself into her work on campus but stopped going to classes. She would drop into Professor Ronald Newton's office to discuss with him the latest news from Central America, but she never did complete his course. She had made up her mind, apparently, that her time was better spent in organizing events and raising awareness about what was happening under the U.S.–backed stewardship of President José Napoleón Duarte. Professor Jorge Garcia, the head of the Latin American Studies program, remembers Christine's constant and vocal presence on campus. He remembers, for example, her appearances before the student council and in the common areas of the school, where she tried to drum up support for the guerrilla cause.

Some of Christine's friends from other courses of study in first year also noticed the change in her. The tall girl with dark, straight hair went from being fairly quiet and always very polite to being both vocal and angry. Her brow furrowed in consternation, her face contorted, she screamed and yelled for action while leading on-campus demonstrations. As Mary Sibierski noted: "It was incredible how quickly she changed. I was really busy with school and studying, but not Chris, she was always at everything, every event — it was nuts."

The university's Latin American Studies Students' Union (LASSU) worked hard to raise awareness and money to help their fellow students in San Salvador. Another person active in the Vancouver scene was Robert (Rob) P. Taylor, the outspoken and brash national tour director for Salvaide, a national aid organization with offices in major centres across Canada. In Salvador, Salvaide was known as "Seeds for El Salvador" and was originally set up as a redevelopment project for the poor of the nation, who hoped to return to their abandoned villages in "zones of conflict," the battlegrounds of the leftist guerrillas' fight. In April 1987, the month after Christine and Keith Hughes visited El Salvador, Taylor and a colleague were arrested by Salvadorean Treasury Police and held for three days in the province of Chalatenango before being ordered out of the country. Taylor recounted the story for readers of *The Peak*, for which he held a media accreditation card.

Taylor brought back to Simon Fraser his firsthand experience of the horror of lurking death squads. He also brought a hard edge and made no effort to hide his belief in the armed struggle being waged by the Farabundo Martí National Liberation Front. The negotiated peace that was being pushed at the United Nations and in Washington did not satisfy him: he felt that the only outcome of the conflict should be the military victory of the guerrillas. In the downtown Vancouver office of Salvaide, the literature and banner of the Farabundo Martí were prominently displayed, and the affiliation between the two groups was well known.

As Christine and Keith Hughes continued to rally on campus, they formed a new group, the awkwardly named Central American Simon Fraser University Students' Association (CASFUSA). It was through her new work with CASFUSA that Christine came to know the student politicians on campus. These were the people who could help her with money, setting up information tables, booking space for rallies, and getting the student council to pass motions condemning the work of Salvador's death squads as part of a political show of support for fellow students in San Salvador. One of the student politicians she came to know was a dynamic young man named Paul Mendes. Although the two were never close friends, they were acquainted and their paths crossed quite often on the small campus. Mendes projected the typical image of the student politician. He toed the left-wing line, calling for more accessible, less expensive university education across the province, and vowing to fight for the elimination of tuition fees altogether. He helped Christine's group out whenever he could, well aware that voter turn-out rates of about 15 per cent among students meant that it was important to win over the student activists if he hoped to run successfully for president of the student union the next year.

Soon after Christine began her work on Co-op Radio, David Spencer came on board to help with the show. He and Keith Hughes had dropped "85 RPM" to turn to more serious material. Others at the station remember Christine and David being part of a gang of people who shared similar views, a group that would go for beers late at night. Their relationship seems to have come about first, through their political activism. David's work on "85 RPM" had led to his involvement with some of the groups that he and Keith had featured on the show, particularly the El Salvador Information Office in Vancouver, and Salvaide. Everyone who remembers David, including Keith Hughes, recalls a young man barely getting by, always watching his money and looking for people he could help with their moving or any other way to earn some quick cash.

While Christine worked feverishly on campus in Burnaby and continued to contribute to "El Salvador Today" at Co-op Radio, David Spencer stepped up the struggle on the streets of Vancouver, graduating from interviewing people on the radio to calling meetings, putting up posters, and leading the chants at protests in the streets. Much of this planning took place at the Vancouver East Cultural Centre, situated on Venables Street in the Commercial Drive area of Vancouver, a community dotted with Salvadorean restaurants and shops opened by refugees. David and Christine, and their colleagues and friends in peace, were becoming regulars there. It seems they both had found their own path towards helping the people of Salvador. Christine's route had taken her there to experience the struggle first-hand and to the classroom, where professors had shared their knowledge. David's path was more grass roots, with its foundation in the stories of refugees struggling with a new nation and a new language. He had a predisposition to levelling the playing field and giving all an equal chance to have their say and decide their own destiny. These were lessons he'd learned from his father around the kitchen table. Given their beliefs, it was almost inevitable that David and Christine would meet somewhere along the path to achieving their similar goals.

Others who worked for Co-op Radio remember that Sergio Olivares Urtubia was also a regular at the Vancouver East Cultural Centre. He had entered Canada in 1979 as a political refugee under the auspices of the United Nations, having fled the military regime of Chile's Augusto Pinochet. Urtubia had been the leader of the Armed Resistance, the militarized faction of the Movimiento de Izquierda Revolucionaria (Movement of the Revolutionary Left), which had plotted secretly to overthrow Pinochet's dictatorship. After being caught, tortured, and imprisoned, Urtubia was later exiled and streamed into a refugee plan that placed him in Canada, his entry sponsored by the federal government under what was called "the South American Special Program."

No one is certain when or where David Spencer first met Urtubia. It could have been in 1982, when they were both living in Winnipeg at addresses that were just three blocks apart. David was barely twenty years old when he lived in Winnipeg and just getting his first taste of personal freedom and political action. Two years later, he was living in Vancouver when Urtubia turned up again, this time to live in a house in East Vancouver, six blocks from where David lived.

In late 1987, Urtubia's neighbours remember, David and Christine often came and went from Urtubia's run-down bungalow. Although it was never officially home to Christine and David, it was described as a "Latin American flophouse" by neighbours, a spot where anybody who needed a place to stay was welcome as long as they were up for a political discussion. The landlord asked few questions, and didn't mow the lawn or spend too much time or money on the upkeep.

It was contact with people such as Rob Taylor, who had been there and experienced the feeling of life inside a Salvadorean prison, and Sergio Urtubia, who had known torture and imprisonment at the hands of a tyrannical government, that friends say led David and Christine to demand to know how they could make a positive contribution. After years of listening to the horror stories of others, Keith Hughes says they yearned to go and see for themselves what it was they were fighting for.

Perhaps Christine should have put a little more stock in the words of Professor Ronald Newton, who remembers telling his students not to overestimate their power to change a culture and a nation about which they knew next to nothing.

"It was a time when there were all sorts of well-intentioned foreigners running about, thinking they could change the world," Newton remembers. "All they really did, for the most part, was get in the way and endanger the lives of the people to whom the struggle really did belong."

All that was happening in their lives seemed to bring Christine and David closer to each other. Without anybody really ever noticing what was going on, the pair went from being friends with shared interests to being lovers with shared passions.

CHAPTER 3

On the Move

Beside David's name and telephone number in her small green address book, Christine drew a row of five tiny hearts. It was not long after they started dating that the phone at David's Salsbury Drive apartment in Vancouver was disconnected, and David moved into Christine's one-bedroom Templeton Avenue apartment in Vancouver East sometime in mid-1987. The young lovers would hold hands under the table during strategy meetings at late-night diners and bars or sit on the ground arm in arm at demonstrations. Although Christine was more than four years older than David, she seemed younger. She giggled almost childishly when David made one of his sarcastic cracks.

As much as he took his work seriously, David was a man who could tell a good joke. With a wry wit and black sense of humour, he was often called upon to introduce speakers and deliver the opening remark at Salvaide rallies, offering a light note from the podium. He and Keith Hughes had roamed Vancouver looking for good material for their radio show and were constantly pointing out the humour in seemingly serious stories that teetered on the verge of the ridiculous. Despite his busy volunteer schedule, David still sought odd jobs to pay the bills and found time to indulge his love of alternative music in the Vancouver band scene. Whenever a band or a familiar face from his punk days in Moncton passed through town, David was in the audience to cheer them on. He and Hughes had features on their program that included the typical young people's fare of "where to get the biggest, best, cheapest meal in town." The two would get so wrapped up in planning their next show that often Spencer and Hughes would miss the last bus home along Hastings Street. Forced to walk home, they would try to hitch rides and were jumped by street people or angry young drunks from Vancouver's meaner streets on more than one occasion. But remembering what he had learned from his conflict with the headbangers at Harrison Trimble High School in Moncton, David could ease the tension in almost any situation and calm people down without much effort. Keith Hughes remembers a tense strategy meeting when David jumped up and suddenly announced that he couldn't go on unless he was promised at least two hours of street hockey after the meeting.

"Dave always played goal. Ken Dryden was the childhood hero for both of us," Hughes said, with a laugh.

Nobody remembers ever seeing David Spencer when he wasn't in control. He would dance in a frenzy to the latest punk bands but never seemed to go wild, even with the music he loved. He always knew his limits, never drank more than a couple of beers, and never displayed a great deal of emotion. Even when he was with Christine, he was restrained. The two rarely embraced in public, despite Christine's affectionate nature. David had shed his black leather wardrobe and adopted a very straight-laced, conservative appearance. He usually wore a crisp shirt and casual pants, and kept his hair short and tidy. With his glasses and conventional clothing, he looked more like an accounting student than a political activist.

Christine was the romantic. She wrote cute love notes to David, always signed with hearts. She raved about him to her girlfriends, always deferred to his intelligence, and said she admired his commitment and his passion for helping others. Friends got the impression she would do anything for him; all he had to do was ask. Few of her friends from her days before Simon Fraser had ever met David. Her devotion to him and to their work had taken her away from them. But the few with whom she stayed in touch said she was certain she had found the man she would love for the rest of her life. As for David, friends say he seemed happy to have a steady girlfriend again. He'd been with his former girlfriend, Sue Cormier, since age seventeen and was used to having someone around. Friends say he really didn't like to be alone.

While David cracked jokes and devoted almost every waking hour to his volunteer work, Christine continued to rely on a regular, every-other-week cheque from one of her parents' companies. It helped cover the cost of rent and food, and gave her time to devote to her causes. When David moved in to share her apartment, the cheque was stretched a little farther to cover the bills for both of them.

Christine told people that she was estranged from her parents, that they didn't know where she lived or what she was doing. Perhaps this was part of the pose she had adopted as a member of the rebellious counter-culture. Or perhaps she thought that she would not be taken as seriously in her fight for the poor and oppressed if people knew she came from a prosperous, professional, conservative family. Most people who worked with Christine on various committees describe her as an angry young woman who had rejected her parents and their "capitalist trappings" and had become her own person, free from the demands of a family that flaunted its money.

Keith and Marilyn Lamont insist that this was never the case. They say that Christine had always been very close to them. She lunched with her mother beside the pool in Langley on a regular basis. She brought home to them her message about the terrible conditions that existed in much of Latin America. She gave them an education about what was really happening there, as opposed to what was making the evening news, filtered and sanitized by American media for domestic consumption.

Whatever it was that Christine was promoting as her public persona, within the confines of the comfortable Lamont home she was the loving daughter she had always been. In their daughter the activist, Keith and Marilyn saw a reinvented version of the little girl who had rallied her two sisters to join in adopting a poor child in India, and who raised money through lemonade stands and bake sales to send to her each month. It was a gratifying sight for parents worried about what their children were doing with their lives.

In the circles in which the Lamonts moved, many parents could boast of their children's worldly success — their acceptance into law or medical school and their embarkation on professional careers. But Keith and Marilyn remained big supporters of their children. They would help them out if they needed it, without the kids even having to ask.

By early 1988, Christine's appearances in class were rare. She announced to her family that she and David planned to move to Toronto at the end of the term, where they would pick up their work with the local offices of Salvaide and the Emergency Committee for El Salvador. They thought that, in Toronto, they would be able to expand their list of contacts in the refugee community while they planned a trip to Central America. Christine told her parents she would resume her studies, enrolling at the University of Toronto. She said she was interested in the possibility of one day entering law school, after her return from Central America. Her area of expertise would be human-rights law. With this assurance, Keith and Marilyn agreed to finance the move east and her continued schooling.

Christine and David packed up her small 1983 Toyota, a gift from her parents, and drove east in the spring of 1988. They looked at the apartments-for-rent section in Toronto's *NOW Magazine* and found a listing for a small one-bedroom apartment on the third floor of an old house on Marion Street in Toronto's Sunnyside area. The rent was $420 a month, and the landlord, Richard Barta, who also lived in the building, remembers there being a steady stream of visitors climbing the stairs to the attic apartment, which contained little more than a bed and some books.

"David was a quiet guy, and Christine was a little more outgoing, a kind of wild type of girl," says Barta. "They had a lot of South American friends who came to visit them. I have no idea where from. I just knew they spoke Spanish with them."

Christine was the administrator in the household. She took care of the bills: an $800 cheque from her parents covered the insurance on the car; a cheque for $417.08 was deposited every two weeks into her account in Langley, which she then transferred to her Toronto account and used to cover other expenses. She received extra cash infusions for car maintenance, and on one occasion a cheque for a new $250 dress. She also took care of David's speeding tickets. She balanced her chequebook to the penny, taking into account every bank service charge.

David was busy working at the Salvaide office that ran out of the Poor Alex Theatre on Brunswick Avenue in Toronto's Annex area. Christine picked up work as a waitress at the Top of Toronto restaurant, the touristy revolving eatery atop the CN Tower. She made no plans to enrol at the University of Toronto.

By the summer of 1988 she and David were getting serious about their trip to Central America. They had joined the volunteer team at Toronto's community radio station CKLN, which runs out of what is today Ryerson Polytechnic University, and were quickly accepted into the local community. Their work with "El Salvador Today" led them to the possibility of work in Managua, Nicaragua, where they could function as translators for the news coming out of Farabundo Martí strongholds in El Salvador. They had also heard about the possibility of translating an underground newspaper called *El Rebelde* (The Rebel). It wasn't the strong contribution they were looking to make, but it would give them a home base and a start.

During their time in Toronto, David and Christine met many people who had escaped Salvador and other troubled nations of Latin America. They also met Byron Darlison, a long-time worker at CKLN Radio. At this time he was a station manager and also ran his own business, Darlison and Associates, refurbishing obsolete computer equipment that was, in turn, sold very cheaply or donated to aid organizations to be shipped to Central America.

Darlison remembers this as a time when refugees would appear on radio programs or arrive for rallies or interviews using false names. There had been accurate media reports to the effect that notorious killers from El Salvador were themselves being granted refugee status and let loose on the streets of Toronto. "It was a time when everyone was a José or a Maria — code names were the norm for those people. They were still scared, even though they were in Canada," Darlison said. He remembers that Christine and David were very busy, organizing speeches and rallies, and that, considering the work David did, "he was the squarest, most straight-looking guy you'd ever seen."

Christine and David's time in Toronto was short-lived. In September 1988, they moved their work with Salvaide to Ottawa and settled in a small apartment on Arlington Avenue, in the neighbourhood known as Centretown. But within two months, they moved to a cheaper apartment in the less desirable west end, on Pinhey Street. It was from this third-floor apartment that Christine Lamont and David Spencer began to construct the lies that they would carry with them to Central America. It was in this apartment that they would plot a course that would land them in a Brazilian jail.

CHAPTER 4

WHO'S WHO

AT SOME POINT IN THEIR CAREERS, FROM DEMONSTRATIONS ON the streets of Vancouver to pushing paper in the Toronto and Ottawa branches of Salvaide and the El Salvador Information Office, Christine and David changed. The closer the time came for them to make their long-anticipated trip to Central America, the more determined they became to make a real difference. Friends from those days say they seemed willing to pay any price to help out in any way possible. They made tentative plans to leave early in 1989, perhaps as early as January. They worked to set up contacts with the Farabundo Martí headquarters in Managua, where they would work as translators, even though it was a job that Christine's Latin American Studies professors say she was ill-equipped to carry out. Professor Newton says there is no way Christine was fluent enough to translate, although she seemed to have picked up some conversational Spanish through her studies.

Between the time of their arrival in Ottawa in September 1988 and Christine's visit home to Vancouver for Christmas that year, the pair worked tirelessly, amassing a remarkable amount of paperwork and shuttling back and forth between Toronto and Ottawa. Byron Darlison, their acquaintance from CKLN Radio, remembers them accompanying refugees to meetings and support rallies in Toronto. "I thought they were still living here. They were here every weekend, it seemed," Darlison said.

Christine and David were keeping busy in both cities. In anticipation of their trip, both obtained Canadian passports on November 2, 1988. One month later, both filed police reports saying they had inadvertently left their new passports in the back seat of a taxi in Ottawa. They applied for and were issued new passports on December 6, 1988.

On December 12, just six days after receiving her second Canadian passport, Christine was issued an American passport, a privilege accorded her by virtue of her having been born in Boston when her father was working there. Despite all Christine's denunciations of U.S. intervention in Central America, she had no aversion to carrying an American passport.

On December 1, Christine and David both were issued press identification for Toronto's *NOW Magazine*. The magazine reports that the pair neither worked there nor wrote for the weekly tabloid-style entertainment paper, but press cards were issued quite readily to would-be writers heading off on an extended trip who expressed a desire to send back stories on a free-lance basis.

A few days later, Christine and David both were issued international drivers' licences, again something that might come in handy in Central America if they were to rent or borrow a car.

A letter dated December 9 on letterhead from a company called Pica Importer in Ottawa stated that David Spencer had worked at the company as an accounting clerk for more than two years. The letter, signed by E.J. Ames, President, said "reliability and quality work are [David's] most outstanding characteristics." David had lived in Vancouver for most of the previous two years, and no one in Ottawa remembers him working as an accounting clerk.

David also obtained a personal letter of reference, dated December 15, 1988, on CKLN stationery, signed by Byron Darlison. The letter reads:

> This letter is to confirm that I have personally known David Spencer for 7 years. I first met David in Vancouver while studying business administration at the University of British Columbia.
>
> Together we were active members of the Business Students' Club and became close friends during our time at school.
>
> As a friend David was always trustworthy and reliable and as a businessman has proven himself to be both innovative and successful. David is keen and continues to be an inspiration to all of those fortunate enough to know and work with him, and I would gladly testify to his outstanding character for anyone requiring a reference.

The problem with this glowing testimonial is that Byron Darlison says he didn't write it. He had known David only a few months at that point, he never attended school in British Columbia, and he had no idea what kind of businessman David Spencer would make because he had never known him to do anything other than his work with Salvaide.

A letter of reference for Christine, also dated December 15, is typed on stationery from Darlison's computer company, Darlison and Associates, and signed by Byron Darlison. This letter states that "Christine Gwen Lamont is on assignment for Darlison Associates and she is hereby authorized to act as our agent in all manner of contracts and other binding agreements. . . ." Byron Darlison didn't write this letter either. Nor did he write the professional reference for David, worded identically with Christine's, that is dated February 21, 1989. Darlison says he also did not hand over the stacks of blank stationery, envelopes, and business cards that Christine and David packed up when they left for Central America. He has no idea how or why the pair took the trouble to obtain these letters of reference making them out to be something they weren't.

In the weeks leading up to Christine's trip home to Langley for Christmas, she withdrew thousands of dollars from her bank account. In addition, her parents had sent money for her airfare home, plus an extra $200 so she could change the date of her ticket, plus a $500 "loan from Mom," as the entry in her cheque register showed.

It was while she was in British Columbia that Christmas that Christine apparently obtained a personal letter of reference from her former professor Ronald Newton. Newton says he doesn't remember writing the letter, but says it is entirely possible that he might have written a Spanish note of introduction. Such letters are a common device employed by those travelling in Central America to overcome language barriers and to make a first contact at a university or with missionaries and aid workers.

If Ronald Newton did write a letter of introduction, it was not the one that Christine took with her. The letter dated December 28, 1988, that accompanied Christine on her trip was written on stationery from the Canadian University Press, a student press news sharing collective. The letter states:

> This is to certify I have known Christine Gwen Lamont for 9 years, first in our relationship as a professor and student and later as a personal friend. As a student, Christine was methodical and thorough in her research, well organized in her presentation material and demonstrated a keen sense of analysis. Christine has since proven her capacity to adapt these qualities for use in her present work.
>
> It has been a pleasure to know Christine and I would be happy to attest to her upstanding personal character at any time. . . .

Professor Newton had known Christine for about two years, and since she did not complete his course, would not have issued such glowing compliments about her academic performance. In fact, the letter would ring somewhat hollow to anyone who knew her. Christine had tried and failed twice as a student. Several people who knew her at Simon Fraser, including Paul Mendes, the former student council president, didn't think Christine was even enrolled as a student in her final year, but was rather using the campus as a base for her political work.

In the early weeks of 1989, Christine and David obtained other references, including one from the Toronto-based International Council of Adult Education. The letter, signed by Lynda Yanz, states that David is doing fieldwork for a project sponsored by the Indigenous Program of the council to research the culture and history of the indigenous people in Central America. Lynda Yanz said she doesn't remember writing the letter on behalf of the CIDA–funded agency. She doesn't even remember having met David Spencer. She said it is possible that she gave the letter to someone who had told her about David Spencer to pass along, thinking it would help open doors for two young human-rights workers heading to Nicaragua, reportedly to do research, but she can't absolutely confirm or deny having written it because the records have long since been archived or destroyed. Yanz also has no idea how David managed to obtain dozens of pieces of blank stationery and envelopes from the council.

Another professional letter of reference came from Teknos Career Institute in Vancouver. It states that Christine and David were looking into the possibility of setting up a business school in Central America.

Both also obtained identification cards stating that they were journalists with CKLN Radio, and press cards from SFU's student publication *The Peak*. They also had business cards and blank stationery for an arts and crafts company in Vancouver called Satoricraft; stationery from an importing company called Artesania Inc. in Ottawa; and stationery from a downtown Vancouver apartment building called the Manhattan Co-op. Other blank stationery came from the Simon Fraser University Department of Political Science, the Simon Fraser student union, Canadian University Press, Teknos Career Institute, and CKLN Radio. Christine also collected stationery from her father's medical practice, with the names of his colleagues, Dr. F.G. Forrest and Dr. D.A. Shirley, listed at the top. The supply of paper also included blank stationery from the family company that had been paying Christine her steady allowance, Lamont Holdings.

Christine and David both received American Express credit cards for their trip, and took along a variety of office supplies, including stencilling equipment, erasers, and glue.

Each had dozens of passport pictures taken over the course of just a few weeks. In each picture, they look a little different. Christine's hair changes from dark brown to light brown to dirty blonde to blonde in the photographs. David Spencer poses with and without his glasses and is dressed in a shirt and tie in some pictures and more casually in others.

Their departure date was now scheduled definitely for the last week of February 1989. By that time, with all the papers and other supplies they had amassed, David and Christine had a lot of luggage for their trip south. They also had a fair amount of money. David had $8,000 in the bank, and they sold Christine's Toyota for extra cash.

Christine packed three passports, David two. They had letters telling people they were everything from academics to computer salespeople, business instructors to importers and working journalists. They did not, however, have a single piece of documentation linking them to a nationally or internationally recognized aid organization, be it Oxfam, Peace Brigades, or Amnesty International. They didn't even have a letter of introduction from Salvaide, the Canadian aid organization for which both had, in fact, done work in the past.

By the time these two young idealists boarded the plane for Panama and Managua, they had already embarked on a journey that would take them a long way from the lives and values that their parents embodied.

CHAPTER 5

A SMOGGY HEAVEN

IN SEPTEMBER 1988, THE SAME MONTH THAT CHRISTINE AND David were setting up house in Ottawa, Sergio Olivares Urtubia, the Chilean exile they knew in Vancouver, slipped back into Chile from Argentina.

It had been eighteen years since Urtubia, along with thousands of others, had celebrated in the streets as socialist Popular Unity (UP) leader Salvador Allende took office as president. Urtubia's joy then had been short-lived. General Augusto Pinochet led the military coup that ousted Allende's government in September 1973, and followed it with a brutal campaign to silence opponents. The ensuing campaign of terror had led to the formation of the Movimiento de Izquierda Revolucionaria (Movement of the Revolutionary Left, or MIR), an anti-government organization which carried out a series of bombings of military targets and sought to impede in other ways Pinochet's autocratic rule. Pinochet's government, meanwhile, embarked on an economic program that entailed, among other things, a massive switch to privatization intended to reverse the work of the Allende government.

Now, in 1988, after having been officially barred from his homeland for ten years, Urtubia was leaving Canada to return to his people and his struggle. Urtubia went home, to San Felipe, a town north of Santiago, to help with preparations for the plebiscite scheduled for October 5, 1988. The vote was meant to give Chile's 7.4 million voters the opportunity to determine whether or not the seventy-two-year-old Pinochet would be handed another eight-year term as president and head of the military.

Urtubia's homecoming, along with that of thousands of other Chilean exiles, reflected an optimistic belief that things were changing for the better, that the MIR's political faction was on the verge of being granted national recognition. There was also evidence that the guerrilla faction, of which Urtubia had been a part before his exile, was once again active. Diplomats in Chile at the time believed the group had re-formed in case Pinochet refused to leave office despite a likely defeat in the national plebiscite. The fear that military rule might once again take on an ugly and dangerous character caused the guerrilla faction to prepare for every eventuality. The result of Urtubia's group's decision to once again gear up not only would affect his fellow Chileans, but also would have long-lasting consequences for Christine and David.

Four thousand kilometres north of Chile, the Managua that greeted Christine and David was, in 1989, a kind of teeming ruin, at once vital and teetering on the brink of collapse. The smell of diesel fuel from the passing buses and the rank exhaust fumes from American cars were a noxious, ever-present reminder of Nicaragua's ten-year-old revolution. The American buses and cars were almost all imported before the July 19, 1979, uprising by the Sandinista National Liberation Front (FSLN) that caused president Anastasio Somoza to flee for Paraguay, his pockets stuffed with $500 million of the people's dollars, much of it the missing aid money sent for earthquake relief seven years earlier.

Nicaragua was embroiled in a civil war. The money and scarce resources that were pumped by the Sandinista government of President Daniel Ortega into keeping the twelve thousand American-trained and -financed Contra soldiers at bay in the border hills of northern Nicaragua had taken a visible toll. Despite the Sandinista efforts to maintain a front of normality, food and fresh water were scarce, guns were everywhere, and inflation ran towards 1,300 per cent a year. The office towers and downtown streets of Managua, which had never been rebuilt after the devastating earthquake in 1972, stood as hollow and crumbling reminders of the country's failures.

The Sandinista government was approaching the brink of financial ruin. Saddled with $5 billion in foreign debt and burdened by an American trade embargo, the nation had grown desperately reliant on Cuba and the Soviet Union to supply arms and much-needed materiels that could not be obtained from other sources. The entire nation of almost four million people, with its Marxist government and open defiance of the world's foremost superpower, was virtually without friends among the nations of Central America. The policies of the Ortega government might as well have been deliberately calculated as an affront to the United States in particular, and then-president Ronald Reagan spent eight years denouncing and subverting the leftist regime.

In the name of solidarity, and as a matter of survival, taking allies where they could find them, Nicaragua opened its borders to those who shared the views of the Sandinistas. They took their inspiration from Augusto Sandino, the revolutionary hero who fought Nicaragua's first Somoza and was shot dead in 1934. Thousands heeded the welcome during the mid-1980s, some deserving of the hospitality, others taking advantage of a favourable situation. The offer from the Sandinistas was clear: a home base, a no-questions-asked policy, and a Nicaraguan passport if there was a past to be hidden or erased. The Nicaraguan Ministry of the Interior, under the charismatic and stocky Tomás Borge, one of the surviving original Sandinistas, boasted a Soviet-trained intelligence branch that could offer a new identity to the brothers-in-arms of the people of Nicaragua.

And so, for those self-styled outlaws and outcasts who devoted their lives to the leftist struggle, Managua was close to heaven. At the very least, this city had become a haven for terrorists who thought of themselves as freedom fighters, for mercenaries willing to fight a battle for a buck, and for activists who knew they could operate with impunity from the suburban streets.

David and Christine were outcasts of a sort, too, though they were essentially the architects of their own fate. Christine was a failed student, a woman of almost thirty who had yet to make a choice in her life, had yet to accept the responsibilities of adulthood, and had yet to learn how to support herself without cash infusions from generous parents.

David, the punk rocker in accountant's clothing, was an angry young man who, despite his obvious intelligence, could not make a commitment to higher education. He thought he already knew all he needed to know. For years, he thought he could change the world by waving a placard. When he realized the futility of this strategy, he was at first embittered, and then determined to find a new way to bring about a society that he thought was right and just. David was about to cross a dangerous line from peaceful protest to active participation in the struggle of another world and another people.

Among the other characters who had taken up residence in Managua were people like Eusebio Arzalluz, a Basque guerrilla who was given a new name and identity by the Nicaraguans. Arzalluz was wanted in Spain for his alleged part in a series of bombings for which the Euzkadi Ta Askatasuna (ETA; literally, "Basque Homeland and Liberty") claimed responsibility. Arzalluz was a key player in the terrorist cell that had waged a twenty-five year campaign of terror that had taken more than seven hundred lives with little other effect than the promotion of paranoia in Madrid. In Managua, Arzalluz lived under the name Miguel Larios Moreno and was the respectable owner of an auto-repair shop called the Taller de Santa Rosa, a wall-enclosed garage compound, complete with four service bays. His was the garage of choice for many of the city's foreign diplomats and aid workers. Moreno's comfortable home, surrounded by a steel fence, was just a few blocks from the repair shop. Some of the other better-known Basques living in Managua worked for Tomás Borge at the Ministry of the Interior, where their experience in counter-intelligence was welcomed by the Sandinista secret police.

Other Managuan businessmen with less than pristine pasts included men like "Guido," the chef at the popular Magica Roma restaurant in the old downtown area of the city, just steps from the Hotel Inter-Continental, the only high-rise to survive the 1972 earthquake, and home of the only functioning elevators in the country of four million people. Guido, whose real name is not known, was in fact the man hunted for pulling the trigger in the 1978 assassination of former Italian prime minister Aldo Moro — another legacy of the Red Brigades. Guido, with his jovial manner, sailor's cap, and toothless grin, had slipped into Managua and a life of quiet comfort and respectability.

Other notables at the time included members of the Palestine Liberation Organization (PLO), Libyan representatives of the government of Colonel Muammar al-Qaddafi, faces from Italy's Red Brigades, and Sergio Urtubia's former allies, the Movement of the Revolutionary Left (MIR).

Another man who sought sanctuary in Nicaragua was Enrique Gorriaran Merlo, code-named "Ricardo." Ricardo spent more than twenty years as a soldier in the Sandinista struggle. But his roots were in Argentina, where he fought for the leftist People's Revolutionary Army. He was one of countless foreigners who made up the Sandinista Front, lured to Nicaragua by the first revolutionary success for Latin Marxists since Cuba in 1959. Ricardo had earned the respect of the Sandinistas and would seek their help when he tried to move his struggle back to his homeland. Many Nicaraguans considered Ricardo to be owed a debt of gratitude. He was the man who had travelled to Paraguay in 1980, tracked down Anastasio Somoza to a luxurious tree-lined street in a well-to-do neighbourhood of the capital of Asunción, and blew him apart with twenty-five bullets from two magazines of his fully automatic M-16 assault rifle. For good measure, Ricardo's Argentine colleagues had fired a rocket from a Chinese-made, hand-held rocket-launcher that blew apart the roof of Somoza's Mercedes, tearing off his chauffeur's head. But Ricardo had already taken care of the day's business, single-handedly assassinating one of the most reviled men in recent Latin American history.

Ever since what most Nicaraguans consider to be that heroic, selfless act (for which the Nicaraguans would later pick up the U.S.$33,000 tab), there had been a place close to the heart of the ruling Sandinistas for the Argentinian extremists. Young leftist Argentines would come to Managua to learn the skills of the killing trade, as well as to collect the arms required to continue their fight on the homefront. Ricardo's faction, which went by the initials ERP, had office space in Managua, and several high-ranking lieutenants also held official posts in Tomás Borge's Ministry of the Interior, alongside Basque and Nicaraguan colleagues.

The ERP's prestige was due to suffer a serious blow shortly after New Year's 1989. In an attempt to put an end to right-wing, military uprisings against elected president Raúl Alfonsín, a gang of about fifty left-wing commandos, led by Ricardo, reconvened in Argentina and stormed the La Tablada garrison of the Argentine army, attacking the one hundred soldiers who were on hand. The raid, the first leftist uprising in Argentina in more than a decade, ended in disaster, with twenty-eight dead guerrillas, seven dead soldiers, and one dead police officer.

As a return to the limelight for the People's Revolutionary Army, the attack had been a publicity nightmare, costing Ricardo, who escaped unharmed, the respect of left-wing allies the world over. His hard-fought battles of yesteryear meant nothing amid the freshly spilled blood of ill-trained and ill-equipped young Argentines, many of them teenage boys and girls, sent in to do the work of seasoned terrorists. Ricardo fled into seclusion, sought both by Interpol, the international policing organization based in France, and by furious colleagues-in-arms, disgusted by what they termed his glory-seeking and sloppy planning.

The remaining members of the People's Revolutionary Army had a great deal of rebuilding to do. Their financial resources had been completely depleted, their reputation muddied. They were looking to rebuild and to make amends. They turned to young men like thirty-three-year-old Humberto Paz and his younger brother, Horácio. The Paz brothers had both been captured, jailed, and tortured during the military rule in Argentina from 1976 to 1983. Both had been lucky not to be counted among the more than eight thousand leftists in Argentina who disappeared off the streets during the military rule. Both knew what the struggle was all about and were willing to give anything in the name of their cause. Police believe both also took part in the failed assault at La Tablada.

The two remained in Argentina, but kept in contact with allies in Managua, where the People's Revolutionary Army remained a force and a collaborator for the cause with representatives of Chile's MIR and Salvador's FMLN, specifically the Fuerzas Populares de Liberación (Popular Liberation Forces), one of five factions that comprised the FMLN alliance.

This volatile mixture of extreme-left revolutionaries is what greeted Christine and David when they began work for Radio Farabundo Martí and SalPress, a Salvadorean news agency, within days of their arrival in Managua. Were they prepared to work among a team of seasoned revolutionaries who had seen untold atrocities committed in the name of their struggle? Probably not, but they thought they knew enough, understood enough, of what these people had suffered to be able to work with them in solidarity, to help them return triumphantly to their homelands.

CHAPTER 6

THE PLAN

DAVID AND CHRISTINE'S PLANNED ONE-YEAR STAY IN MANAGUA would be cut short. It was March 1989 by the time they are thought to have started work, although to what extent they actually worked as translators is not known. The couple shared a Managua house with several other FMLN workers and kept in regular phone contact with the Lamonts. Despite Christine and David's savings and the money she had already borrowed from her parents, Christine called them after just two months, asking for more to help pay the rent. She told her parents she and David had not anticipated that the inflation in Nicaragua would be as high as it was, and that their resources were quickly dwindling.

For Christine's birthday on April 21, her parents sent her a small painting by their friend Peter Ewart and a few trinkets and supplies for their work. Christine had asked for erasers, as well as soap, toothpaste, and some cosmetics that were difficult to find in a Managua that was painfully short of consumer goods. The baby-blue card with a childish birthday riddle which Marilyn chose was a glowing testament to her love for their adventure-seeking daughter.

The card, complete with cartoon characters and smiling faces, contained the following notes from members of the family: "To our dear Christy Wisty, with all our love and wishes that your most cherished dreams come true. We're proud of you and our love and thoughts are with you always. I hope this is a very happy and safe day for you and that the day ahead brings happiness and satisfaction. Mom and Dad." The back of the card included hellos from Glenda, son Mark's companion — "Hi Chris, hope you're having a great time and you're having a good birthday. I really miss you. I hope you're doing what you want. May this year be the best yet. Love you lots and happy birthday. Say hi to Dave, Love Glenda . . ." — and from Mark — "Hi, Chris, hope things are going great for you. We miss you, think of you often. I will write a letter updating you on the current events soon, but in the meantime have a happy birthday and stay happy and healthy! Love Mark."

It is difficult to say whether or not Christine Lamont was happy and satisfied on her birthday in Managua. She and David were meeting people who lived in a world that was far removed from Langley, B.C. — with terrorists and extremists from around the globe who felt they had nothing left to lose. An acquaintance of Christine's from Simon Fraser's Latin American Studies program, Professor Jorge Garcia, described terrorists as people who have probably seen too much, and lost so much that they're willing to risk everything in the name of their cause: "The mind of an international terrorist is such that they are willing to put their life on the line. In order for a person to become a terrorist they really have to have suffered something, either they have to be crazy or have been a victim and think to themselves, 'I have nothing else to live for.' "

People who had lived through coups, who had seen their families dragged from their homes, tortured, murdered, or thrown in jail for no legitimate reason, these were people who were candidates to become terrorists. It is the arbitrary and brutal exercise of power that breeds the pure hatred and unadultered drive for vengeance that reveals itself in acts of seemingly senseless violence directed against innocent civilians. In effect, the terrorists turn to their own account the tactics of those who are their enemies. A part of a terrorist's soul has been numbed by what he or she has experienced.

There is no doubt that Managua was a hotbed of this sort of plotting and a home to these types of extremists. For years, such extremists, like the Nicaraguan government that gave them sanctuary, were encouraged and supported by the nations of the eastern bloc. But, as the 1980s rolled by, that support began to wane. Economic crises, the first stirrings of civil unrest prompted by Mikhail Gorbachev's *glasnost*, and other changes indicated that the status quo was about to be upset. One result of these changes was a bizarre and remarkable coming together of terrorist factions. A meeting was convened in Hamburg, Germany, in early 1988 to address the growing problems posed by declining subsidies for the purchase of arms, travel, and underground operations. There was no shortage of arms on the market. The Chinese, and, of course, American arms dealers were ready and waiting to service the terror-purveyors of the world. Whatever the source, materiel was available on a "Pay up, no questions asked" basis: the problem was coming up with the money, and there is always a surcharge for silence.

International authorities have only sketchy details about what transpired at the meeting in Hamburg. They suspect that it was attended by leading members of the Basque separatist movement, who had set up shop in both Managua and Mexico; by Sandinistas, who, despite their status as official government, still are believed to have kept a steady hand in the activities of the extreme left; the Libyans; and the Palestinians. The People's Revolutionary Army, about to reappear on the world stage with the débâcle at La Tablada army garrison, was in attendance, as was the leadership of Chile's Movement of the Revolutionary Left; concerned about what might happen after the plebiscite in October 1988 if Augusto Pinochet was voted out of office by the will of the people and refused to go, this latter group had to be ready to pick up where it had left off in the mid-1970s. Also sitting around the table in Hamburg were representatives from El Salvador's Farabundo Martí (FMLN). Even though they were still in Canada when this meeting took place, Christine and David had already established direct ties with two of the groups represented. Through Salvaide, which was an active and vocal supporter of the FMLN, and through their connection to Chilean Sergio Urtubia, Christine and David had links with this underworld. Police would later conclude that their decision to cross the line, to take the step from activist to extremist, followed the Hamburg meeting. It was then that they began to amass their collection of passports and papers that gave them a variety of identities and suggested that they were willing to lead criminal lives.

Who prompted Christine and David to begin their extensive and illegal collection of Canadian passports and papers has not been determined. The plan could have resulted from their acquaintance with Sergio Urtubia or through their Farabundo Martí contacts in Managua. Before they left Canada, it might not have been clear to Christine and David why they were being asked to bring these documents with them, and it is even possible that they didn't see the harm in what they were doing, that they did not then comprehend where their actions were leading them. Their lies, thefts, forgeries, and deceptions might have represented to them merely small acts of solidarity with oppressed peoples.

It might not have been until some weeks after their arrival in Managua that they began to appreciate the scope of what they were involved with. Perhaps only the hothouse atmosphere of post-revolutionary Managua enabled them to begin to understand the depth of commitment on the part of the people with whom they were dealing.

Other people working in Managua at the time on behalf of human rights — including missionaries and workers with aid organizations — remember tapping into a sense of social justice, a feeling that the people committed to working in Managua were morally superior to other people and were united in opposition to the bullying United States. The atmosphere in Managua then was very supportive, and everyone agreed with everyone else. The thousands of foreigners living in the country shared similar political ideologies, which bred a collective sense that they were doing the right thing. Christine and David may have been swept up in the name of a good cause as they met more and more people whom they trusted and whose opinions they respected. And these people were now asking them to put down their placards and petitions and to pick up arms in the name of solidarity. What is known for sure is that Christine and David heeded the call.

Police in Brazil reported that Christine and David had spent time in a Sandinista training camp, learning the finer points of weapons handling and close combat. The Sandinistas also boasted an intelligence training centre, capable of instructing young recruits on surveillance, disguises, and false identities. By the time Christine and David reportedly underwent training, they must have known the part they were scheduled to play in the larger plan that had been worked out in Hamburg.

The plan was a simple one, and in its implementation showed a remarkable degree of cooperation and forethought. Led in large part by the Basques, the small convention agreed to band together in a fund-raising effort. Each faction would provide its expertise to squads of terrorists who would, in turn, kidnap some of Latin America's most powerful people and hold them for ransom. The money paid out by the families of the distraught victims would be split up between the various groups involved. It would then be used to finance their separate struggles and would offset the loss of funding from the Soviet Union and its surrogates in the East.

No detail was overlooked and no expense spared in preparation for the kidnappings. Police forces in several countries concluded that potential targets were identified using articles in business magazines that outlined the successes of prominent individuals and families. Further research at libraries uncovered quarterly reports, stock sheets, and other details about the financial health of large companies and their presidents, chairmen, and owners. Teams were dispatched to the home towns of the potential targets to begin surveillance. The daily routines of potential victims were documented, including such details as when they left for work each day, the route they took, the security they relied on. The number of their bodyguards was noted, as was the existence of electrified fences around their estates and the presence of bullet-proof glass in the windows of their limousines.

A list of more than a hundred potential targets was narrowed down to the dozen or so most likely to be successfully abducted and ransomed. The criteria included the family's ability to pay, their net worth, and their ability to access the cash without having to liquidate stock and other assets, which might tip off the authorities, who were to be kept out of any negotiations. Other criteria included the public's perception of the target — whether or not the kidnapping would outrage the people and eventually turn sympathies against the terrorists' cause. Points of interest included whether or not the individual was liked by his employees, faithful to his wife, a good father to his children.

All the information about the targets was detailed in typed, well-kept files in a Basque house in Managua that was serving as headquarters for the kidnapping plan. Among the candidates for abduction were Mexican TV tycoon Emilio Azcarraga, who was described in the files as being "hated by society. He treats his workers poorly. He is arrogant." Hotel-chain owners Pablo and Israel Brener were reportedly seen writing a cheque for $6 million, indicating that they were not short of cash to meet a ransom demand. Lebanese immigrant Carlos Slim Helu, who lived in a mansion in Mexico City's Lomas Chapultepec district, had a garbage truck go by his home every morning at ten o'clock, causing the guards to open the front gates, the idea being that, at 10:00 a.m. every day, kidnappers could gain access to the property and their victim. Another Mexican, Lorenzo Servitje, "has social prestige. Nationalist. It would have a social cost." Food magnate "Ignacio Aranguren — he has a lot of money. Very much loved by his family. Would negotiate."

A list of potential targets in Ecuador included the family of Ecuadoran president Sixto Durán Ballén. The Ballén file contained a complete family tree and placed the family's worth at $200 million to $250 million. "Amount to negotiate: $10 million, but could be more with negotiations." Research into the Ballén targets included testing escape routes from Quito to the Colombian border, several hours' drive away. The route was tested four times to determine how often cars are stopped for security checks.

Of the twelve men on the short list whose lives were documented in minute detail, several would later become actual kidnapping victims. One of them, Antonio Gutierrez Prieto, a hotelier and one of Mexico's richest men, was photographed as he went to church for a Mass in honour of his late wife, who had died two years earlier. His young son was abducted within weeks, and held for eight months.

Despite the proliferation of kidnappings in Mexico — as many as five hundred in 1988 alone — it was on Brazilian targets that the terrorists pinned their hopes, planning to carry out the most daring of abductions and to demand the highest of ransoms. The names of two Brazilian men were on the short list. One was an advertising executive named Luiz Salles. The other was a supermarket magnate named Abílio dos Santos Diniz.

CHAPTER 7

GREETINGS FROM MANAGUA

BY MAY 1989, INTERNATIONAL POLICE FORCES, REPRESENTED BY the Paris-based umbrella organization known as Interpol, believe that Christine and David had been selected as the Salvadorean Popular Liberation Forces' contribution to an abduction team that would operate in Brazil. The millionaire Luiz Salles was to be snatched off the street that coming summer, and it is likely that David and Christine were meant to have a role in the abduction.

Salles, the head of Brazil's third-largest advertising agency, was in fact abducted in broad daylight by other members of Christine and David's cell. He was held for sixty-five days in a tent in a field on the outskirts of São Paulo. He was released unharmed in October 1989 only after his family paid U.S.$2.5 million to his captors.

As Canadians, Christine and David would no doubt have been useful in setting up the kidnapping. Coming from a country with a long and respected history of peace and good government, they would draw little attention at border crossings. They were young and looked perfect in the role of university students setting out to see the world. From the point of view of the terrorists, it's easy to see that the Canadians were valued members of the team. But in late May 1989, the two received word that David Spencer's mother, Jean, was near death, and the pair hastily returned to Canada via Costa Rica and Panama. David went immediately to console his distraught father in New Brunswick, while Christine joined her family in British Columbia. Any other plans the pair had were put on hold.

Besides visiting her family, Christine had other errands to tend to during her three-week visit to Langley. The three passports she had already acquired — the first Canadian one, which she had reported stolen but still had in her possession; the replacement passport; and the American passport she had been issued — would not be enough. Christine needed another passport, authentic, but ideally in the name of somebody who had never been involved with the far left, someone whose name would not come up in a computer search at a U.S. or Canadian border point. For the job facing them in the months ahead, David would also require another identity.

Just days after her return to Canada, Christine contacted an old family friend, Lisa Lynne Walker, a woman who had been in the same class at school as Christine's younger sister Heather, and was good friends with the entire Lamont family. Lisa Walker lived in a comfortable house with her husband, Jack, and two young sons, Lee and Dustin. By all accounts the Walkers are a close, loving family, and Lisa a devoted mother who went to school part-time while raising her young family. On June 12, 1989, Lisa Walker travelled from her Aldergrove home, midway between Abbotsford and Langley, to the Vancouver passport office and applied for a Canadian passport for the first time. If Lisa Walker was planning a trip, she told no one, and she did not hand in an application for her husband or request that her children be added to her own passport, as is usually done.

Christine visited Lisa Walker in the course of her visit home. The two women reminisced, gossiped, and looked through old photo albums for an entire afternoon. When Christine left to return to her parents' home in Langley, she was carrying Lisa Walker's newly acquired passport. Christine's collection of passports now numbered four.

During the course of her visit to the Vancouver area, Christine also met with Paul Mendes, the student politician she had got to know through her activities on the Simon Fraser campus. By coincidence, Mendes had also recently acquired a passport, from the same Vancouver passport office from which Lisa Walker had obtained hers. Mendes had made plans for a summer trip to visit relatives in Portugal. Christine and Mendes played catch-up and chatted in an East Vancouver café, and Mendes invited Christine to a small party he was holding at his apartment on Powell Street the following Saturday night. Christine attended the party alone and when she left she was carrying Mendes's newly acquired passport, which had been removed from a briefcase sitting on the floor of his bedroom. Her collection now numbered five.

Christine's visit with her family was a happy one. She picked up the birthday presents that she had not been home to receive in April, including outfits with matching earrings from sisters Elisabeth and Heather. David, meanwhile, mourned his mother and would later remark on his family's ability to pull together in hard times — testimony, he said, to the power of loved ones to cope in the face of adversity and tragedy. But despite the importance of time spent with loved ones, both told their families that they were committed to returning to Nicaragua and resuming their translation work. Both also said that they would have to find a new place to live when they returned to Managua, so they couldn't leave a mailing address behind. They also warned their families that sending packages probably wasn't a good idea because they would take too long to arrive and might be stolen en route, this despite the fact that Christine had received parcels from the Lamonts during her initial stay in Managua. Both promised their families that they would to try to make it home for Christmas. Before setting out again in mid-June, both Christine and David had more passport pictures taken.

They flew back to Managua via Mexico, using their real passports, their own names. Their airplane included an entourage of more than thirty journalists who were accompanying the advance delegations of foreign officials who would act as independent observers in the elections in 1990. Most observers at the time, in mid-1989, were convinced these elections would extend the rule of the Sandinistas once again. In fact, when voting day arrived, it was the hastily organized centre-based coalition led by Violeta Chamorro that soundly defeated Daniel Ortega's Sandinistas. Also on their flight was the actor and singer Kris Kristofferson, who was heading to Nicaragua to make a film about Augusto Sandino. It was a coincidental brush with stardom that Christine would later write home about.

Christine and David did a lot of writing home in the first few days after their return to Nicaragua. As part of their commitment to the cell of Marxist terrorists in Managua, the pair knew that they would be unable to stay in touch with their families after they entered the underground world that awaited them. They would have to focus entirely on the task of raising millions of dollars to support the struggle, to support the FMLN rebels in the hills of Salvador, providing them with desperately needed arms. As they sat in a safehouse in Managua, owned by a Basque exile, they plotted their deception and planned their lies. Christine, in keeping with her habit of being attentive to detail, the same habit that made her balance her chequebook to the penny, kept a list of the lies she and David would be telling their families back home. The lies would be necessary to cover their tracks — to conceal their activities — from the people who knew and cared about them. Their tracks would lead them first to Brazil, then on to Argentina to a rendezvous with other members of their cell, and then back again to Brazil, where their victim awaited them. Christine seemed to have learned along the way that a good liar requires a good memory. She used cheat notes.

Both she and David wrote letters to their families that they would leave with a colleague in Managua, complete with mailing instructions in Spanish saying what month the letters should be sent on to Canada. The letters ran in two-month intervals from July 1989, just weeks after their visit home, until July 1990.

Fake letters are difficult to write. David and Christine had to avoid scrupulously any mention of specific places, names, dates and, of course, world events. The only way to avoid being caught in their lies was to keep the letters short and as general as possible. If they asked a lot of questions about their families back home, they wouldn't have to talk about their own lives. With these considerations in mind, Christine wrote loving, flowery notes to her family. In her July 1989 letter, she talked about everything being more or less the same as when they had left Managua and about how inflation was always on the rise, and she reminisced about her recent visit home:

> For the first few days after we got back I was quite sad and lonely for all of you. It's very much on my mind that I wouldn't be seeing you for quite awhile. I was also running across everything you guys had given me while we were there and indulging myself in a lot of missing you. With David around though and getting back to work, I feel a lot better. So while I'm still thinking about you a lot, I'm thinking about how nice it was to get a chance to see you, that Bone [Christine's nickname for her father, Keith] will soon be on the courts, that Mom will soon be off for the summer, that Beth is involved in a new romance, that Heather and

Franco are bound to have stories to tell me about The Who concert, that it won't be long before Mark and Glenda are off on holidays. Anyway, it was great to see you and it won't really be "that" long before we meet again. Take care everybody, I love you and miss you all. Love Chris.

The farther ahead the letters reached, the more vague the pair had to be in their descriptions of their phoney lives. In the letter that David wrote to his father for March 1990, he does not make a single reference to any named place, person, or event:

Hello Dad, I hope this letter finds everything and everyone well up north. It's just a little after 10 at night, we just got home from working and to be honest are about to fall asleep but I thought I should write you a quick note as I've been procrastinating of late. Not to try to make too many excuses for this but we've really been up to our eyeballs in work for about the last month. We're making some changes here and there and it's turned out to be very time consuming. It's only at times like this when we come even within a mile of complaining about what we're doing and it really isn't the work but rather sometimes you get a little worn out and frustrated when simple things take you too long to get done. Bare [*sic*] with me as I go on a rant. I spent more time today on the phone than I care to admit making a few phone calls. The only problem was most of the places I had to contact I didn't have the numbers for so I had to use the white pages and the yellow pages a lot. Seems simple enough so far? Right. Well, it is until you take into account the last phone book published for this city was about five years ago. Get the picture? In any case, we're still really liking the work a lot and seem to have fit in fairly well. There's no sign of moving away from here for sometime but you never know.

We're thinking it might not be too much longer now until we can pull off a little trip up north. Nothing firm, mind you, but a possibility. Well, I'm getting really tired I should go, thanks for listening and I'll write you again soon. Send my love to everyone. Christine (who has fallen asleep) says hi. Love, Dave.

In other letters, Christine mentions stumbling across an English copy of Fyodor Dostoyevsky's *Crime and Punishment*, a novel she highly recommends to her family back home.

In each letter, David and Christine refer to their "work," but they never once say where they do it or what it is. They couldn't talk about their neighbourhood because they didn't have one. Nor could they refer to their friends by name, or the various towns they claimed to visit for weekend excursions. On the list of stories that Christine kept, she made a notation for the May 1990 letter indicating that both she and David were to "intimate we are in different house." That's exactly what Christine said in that letter.

"Hi Mom and Dad, Beth, Heather, Mark and Glenda, Hi, how are you all. Well I guess by the time you get this it will be close to a year since we saw you last. Sometimes it feels like a lot longer than that and other times it seems like it really couldn't have been more than a few months ago. Thinking back, a lot has happened in that time and I guess it really does constitute a landmark of some kind. Anyway, I've been looking at the pictures I have of all of you and wondering what changes I can expect. Nothing too drastic, I hope. We are starting to try and work out a plan whereby we may be able to get up there for a visit. It's looking pretty good but a little early to say, maybe this summer or for Christmas if not then. In any case, don't be altering any plans, we'll let you know in advance what becomes of our

> scheming. Things are much the same as they were at this time last year. Everyone is getting ready for the rainy season and frankly this time around I'm kind of looking forward to it. The storms can be pretty destructive sometimes but the lightening [*sic*] and thunder and the clouds and the winds are something to be experienced. Reports are too that our roof in this house we're in now doesn't leak. Still, the draw-back, nothing can be done to keep those dastardly bugs out. What else? We were prepared for the Semana de Sante [Easter Week] this time so we won't be caught off guard. Of course, there wasn't much to do in the city so we were off to the beach for the weekend. It was crowded and expensive compared to here but all in all we had fun. So, Bone, I want to wish you a happy Father's Day I wish I were better able to convey how I feel about this but I want you to know how much I love you and what a great friend you are to me. I'll be thinking of you on Father's Day and missing you as much as I am right now. I love you very, very much . . .

The letter that would later offer up the greatest irony in Christine and David's saga was written in July 1989, to be sent to Christine's family in January 1990. The letter read: "How are you all, how was Christmas and how are you all enjoying the 1990s so far. As I had predicted, I missed you all very much at Christmas but all the same, Dave and I had one we won't soon forget. Christmas Eve we spent with two families . . . the next day we had a big turkey dinner at noon, a little different than I expect your bird was, before going to the beach for the afternoon." Christine goes on to describe the wild party they attended on New Year's Eve in an open-air square in the city. She raves about the food, the music, and the dancing.

Sitting in Managua, in July 1989, David and Christine devised their plan to deceive their families, to have the people who loved them think they were living and working in Nicaragua, complete with its awful mail system and the poor telephones that made contact difficult. They tried to alleviate both worry and suspicion before leaving the country for Brazil. Their confident plan, their deception of the people who loved them, shows that they did not even contemplate the possibility that they might get into trouble.

Christine and David would indeed have a Christmas that they wouldn't soon forget. It was spent in solitary confinement in damp, uncomfortable prisons in São Paulo.

CHAPTER 8

PAUL AND LISA

AT THE END OF JUNE 1989, JUST DAYS AFTER THEIR RETURN FROM Canada, David and Christine flew from Managua to Panama. This time they took out their new set of passports and assumed the identity of Lisa Lynne Walker and Paul Joseph Gomez Mendes when they applied for ninety-day visitors' visas to Brazil. They had made still more additions to their collection of false papers while in Managua, creating Ontario drivers' licences in their new names. David had meticulously practised Paul Mendes' signature as it appeared in his passport. Since Lisa Walker had not bothered to sign hers, Christine had signed the document in her own handwriting.

Both used their international drivers' licences, issued in Ottawa the previous November, as a guide in creating a second set in the names of Walker and Mendes. They also wrote letters of reference for Walker and Mendes, using the vast selection of blank stationery they had acquired in Ottawa. To their cache of fake ID, they added student cards and press passes, also newly penned with their false names. Back in Managua, they left behind all traces of their former selves, including a cardboard box containing their extra passports, credit cards, ATM cards, address books, plane tickets — anything in the names Christine Gwen Lamont and David Robert Spencer — in order to avoid any chance that they could be identified after they fled Brazil.

The letters home were put in air-mail envelopes. On pastel-coloured Post-It notes attached to the front of each one, Christine indicated in Spanish, in her round, girlish handwriting, the month in which each letter was to be sent to an address in either Langley or Moncton.

Did Christine consider the possibility of something going wrong? What if the letter for January 1990, in which she described her amazing Christmas day, was actually sent off in November by mistake? How would she explain this? It seems these thoughts didn't even cross her mind as she tucked the crucial foolscap sheet on which she had carefully listed her lies, and David's, in among her other belongings to be left in Managua. She really couldn't afford to lose that piece of paper, but for security reasons and in order to follow part of the plan worked out around that terrorists' conference table in Hamburg, she couldn't risk taking it with her to Brazil.

They arrived in São Paulo sometime in early July and made first contact with their fellow gang members. It is not known what Christine and David did during their early days in Brazil. Neither of them spoke Portuguese, which leads police to believe that they lived with someone who spoke either English or Spanish. Some reports placed them in the north of the country, undergoing further training for their upcoming mission. Other reports suggest that they may have been providing support to the Salles kidnappers, supplying them with food and other necessities. The Salles kidnapping, which would not net a great deal of money in the end, was seen as a dry run, a test case of sorts for the entire gang. The ransom would be used mainly to finance larger, much more lucrative kidnappings in the months and years ahead.

Christine and David bought a white Volkswagen Kombi minivan under their false names. Police believe this was the van used to travel back and forth repeatedly between São Paulo and several different border crossings, keeping careful record of the time it took, the amount of fuel required, the number of police cars they passed, and any security checks they may have encountered along the way. Again, police think it was Christine's habit of paying attention to detail that came in handy for this crucial task of planning escape routes. Where they got the money for the van is not known since neither of them had a large savings account.

In mid-July, they travelled to Argentina, where another meeting of the cooperative of terrorists involved in the kidnapping plot was convened. Progress reports were given on the ongoing campaign in Mexico, Ecuador, and Brazil. To the initial dossiers compiled in Managua, details had to be added in the weeks leading up to the kidnappings. Exact schedules had to be pinned down, along with phone numbers. Who would be the best person to demand as a negotiator for the families involved? Where were the victims to be kept? This initial planning work was done by what was known as the first team. The second team would secure the hiding spot and take care of the logistics. The third team would carry out the kidnapping itself, handing off the victim to the second team, which would then be responsible for taking care of him while the third team assumed the role of negotiator. The Salles plan had been risky and logistically difficult. It worked in the end, but it was not ideal. The plan to keep him in a tent was a poor one, as the police could have easily tracked them down, and the negotiations had taken far too long. For the bigger fish, for Abílio dos Santos Diniz specifically, the supermarket vice-president with massive personal wealth, better arrangements would be required. The police effort that would go into finding Diniz would be like nothing Brazil had ever seen before, and the kidnappers had to be ready.

Humberto Paz, code-named Juan Carlos, one of the men who

had emerged among the leaders of the People's Revolutionary Army, was in charge of the Diniz operation. In Argentina he assigned specific tasks. Christine, code-named Susanna, and David, code-named Modesto, would be leaders of the second team. Christine and David would provide the safehouse where some of the kidnappers would live while finalizing plans and where the victim, code-named Carmelo, would be kept following the operation.

By mid-August, Christine and David were back in São Paulo. On August 17, they both signed a lease using their assumed names for a large house on a suburban street, 295 Rúa Francisco Pugliesi. They moved in right away and wasted no time in making changes designed to discourage interest on the part of neighbours. David bought planks and other materials so that the workmen who would soon arrive could cover the windows. Locksmiths and masonry workers arrived to put up tall gates and build a wall around the front of the house. Large planters were brought in to camouflage the front of the house and the garage door. Curious neighbours looked on during these deliveries, suspicious that the new couple were involved in drug trafficking. They remember that the work took several weeks, with David supervising, explaining to the workers in a mixture of broken Portuguese and Spanish what had to be done and what improvements were required, and expressing satisfaction with or criticism of the job. The work on the gates did not at first satisfy David, who objected loudly to a five-centimetre gap between the swinging gate and the gatepost; furious, he departed from his usual calm, controlled manner and loudly ordered it closed, a conversation overheard by several neighbours. As the weeks before the kidnapping was due to take place zipped by, David seemed to be getting anxious. In the macho world of Latin America, it was to him, not Christine, that the others looked for leadership. It was at him that the finger of blame would be pointed if something went wrong.

Despite David's best efforts, something did go wrong. The

house on Rúa Pugliesi turned out to be totally unsuitable. There always seemed to be São Paulo police cars on the tiny road, for no obvious reason. It turned out that a policeman and his family lived right across the street, and his colleagues were often in the area and stopped in. Because of this unanticipated complication, plans would have to be delayed; the others scheduled to arrive and share the house with Christine and David would be told to hold off, to stay in their holding places, whether they were in Argentina, Chile, Nicaragua, or elsewhere in Brazil.

The search for a house began anew. This time, the plotters settled for a mid-sized suburban home in a different part of the city, far away from Rúa Pugliesi. "Lisa" told her neighbour on Rúa Pugliesi that she and "Paul" were leaving the country, returning to Holland, something the neighbours found strange since Lisa had told them days before that they were expecting others to arrive soon to share the large house and expensive rent. But "Lisa" said an emergency had arisen: her mother had been diagnosed with cancer. In fact, the pair were travelling no farther than another district of the city, just leaving the neighbourhood two and a half months into a prepaid six-month lease.

From Rúa Pugliesi, Christine and David moved straight into the second house at 149 Praca Hachiro Miyazaki, on October 30. David, as Paul Mendes, signed a lease for the two-storey residence on a small street, across the road from a parkette. As proof that they had the money to pay the rent, David used his collection of blank stationery to produce a letter of reference from the Vancouver jewellery importing company, Satoricraft, stating that he, Paul Mendes, was a buyer for the company.

Once again there was work to be done around the new house. David made trips to the store for construction supplies, including cement and wood, which neighbours remember seeing him carry to the rear of the house from the couple's white Kombi van. They bought a striped canopy that shielded much of the front of the house. Several large potted palm trees blocked the view from the street without being too obvious. Christine kept herself busy coming and going with groceries and other supplies, and talking to the neighbours, asking questions about who lived in the neighbourhood.

The delay caused by having to vacate the first house meant that both David and Christine had to renew their ninety-day visas in São Paulo. Only one visa extension can be obtained within the country for foreigners who do not have a permanent work permit or a job of some sort. David went to Uruguay in late November; Christine travelled to Argentina just days later. On her quick trip to Argentina, Christine would risk a phone call to her family to wish her sister Heather a happy birthday and alleviate for the moment her family's worries about her welfare. They had not been receiving her letters from Managua and were, indeed, concerned about her. She told them she and David were on a brief holiday to Argentina. She made no mention of Brazil.

Both Paul and Lisa were safely back in the country on December 11, the morning that Carmelo — the man who had unknowingly been the subject of much scrutiny for several months — was jolted in the driver's seat of his Mercedes when it was struck from behind by a white van.

PART II:
THE CRIME

CHAPTER 9

SNATCHED

THE NOISE WAS DEAFENING. THE TREMBLING, SWEATY MAN thought it was coming from somewhere up high in the room, but in the pitch darkness he had no way of knowing. It was Brazilian country-and-western music being played at full volume, and every drum beat seemed to pound away at his sanity. Along with his wits, Abílio Diniz was clinging to the small pillow he'd been given as he lay on a thin foam mattress inside his tiny cubicle. He had tried to stand up, to feel his way around the room, but wherever he reached his tall frame hit a wall or the ceiling. The ever-pounding music quickly disoriented him, propelling him back onto his makeshift bed.

He was alone — that he knew. If he'd had company in his tiny cell, he would have been able to sense, perhaps even smell, them. His jumbled thoughts ran in every direction. He wondered if he would see his family again. The faces of his two tiny granddaughters came to mind, and that of his nineteen-year-old son who was trying to make it on the amateur car-racing circuit but had yet to win a race. Diniz thought also of his ageing father who had passed on control of the family Pão de Açucar grocery-store chain to him with such trust and optimism. Pão de Açucar, Portuguese for "Sugarloaf," was the ninth-largest private company in Brazil, with 522 stores nation-wide and earnings in 1988 of more than U.S.$2 billion. Abílio, its youthful executive vice-president, was one of Brazil's best-known millionaires. As he fought off morbid thoughts of dying inside this loud, crude box, Abílio Diniz tried to work out what he had done to deserve this. What was his crime? Had he not been a good father? A good son? Indeed, a good employer to more than 45,000 people in Brazil? Whom had he hurt? He had money. Was that all it took to end up alone and scared in a cave, with just the blaring of frivolous music for company?

By the time they had cut him out of the chicken wire that bound his arms and wrists, the events in the morning hours of Monday, December 11, 1989, had changed Abílio Diniz forever.

After an early breakfast, he had dressed impeccably, as always, in a double-breasted business suit, accessorizing with cuff-links, a tie clip, and a handgun tucked in a holster under his arm. He walked briskly out the front door of his home on the posh Rúa Sabuji and climbed behind the wheel of his white Mercedes-Benz S-series sedan, licence number PS2220. It was 8:10 a.m., and Abílio was on schedule. Barring traffic that was worse than usual in the cluttered, dirty streets of São Paulo, he would arrive at his corporate head office in air-conditioned comfort by no later than 9:00 a.m.

As he set out, Abílio was no doubt thinking that this day would be different from his usual routine. On this day, Abílio was set to launch his new book. Although not a writer, he had decided the time had come to record his theories on economic success and discuss the methods for solving Brazil's economic ills, particularly its rampant inflation. The timing could not have been better. Since taking over full control of his company, Abílio had more than tripled net profits from the previous year. He was on a roll, and looking to the future. His optimism was reflected in the title of his new book — *Economic Reform for Brazil in the 1990s*. The work itself, completed with the help of a ghost writer, was textbook-like in its precision but presented with a glossy, steamy novel–type cover. Given Abílio's business success, publishers had no doubt that anything he put his name to would be a best-seller.

As Abílio pulled away from the front door and passed through the security gates in front of his house, a man standing less than a hundred metres away nodded his head vigorously at the car with licence plate PS2220, a gesture that Abílio did not notice. On this morning, Abílio's ride in the Mercedes would last only the five hundred metres from his house to the intersection of Rúa Sabuji and Rúa Serido. There he was cut off by a speeding ambulance and, at the same moment, rear-ended by a white, four-door German-made Opel driven by a woman. With a mere nod of the head, the dark-haired man in sunglasses standing on the street corner had triggered a reign of terror on the rich of Brazil, and the worst moments of Abílio Diniz's life.

Abílio understood the danger he was in the minute his car was boxed in. The driver's door of the Mercedes was flung open and a man in what looked like a military policeman's uniform reached for Abílio with his left hand. In his right hand, he held a pistol. Abílio pulled back his suit jacket to reveal to his attacker that he, too, was armed. The would-be policeman, now accompanied by three others, all armed with handguns, were undeterred and hauled him from the car. Abílio had no chance to draw his gun and defend himself. He realized instantly that he was hemmed in on all sides and that any exchange of gunfire would probably cost him his life. Instead, he more or less passively absorbed at least three hard blows to the head, one with the butt of a handgun. It was enough to keep him off balance as he was dragged into the rear of the waiting ambulance.

From his viewpoint behind the steering wheel of his car across the intersection, Armando Da Silva sat and shook with fear as he saw the gunmen drag the well-dressed man "like a sack of potatoes" and throw him into the white van. Da Silva, a private chauffeur who had been approaching the intersection when he heard the screeching tires of Abílio's attackers, slid down behind the steering wheel of his own car and prayed the men would not notice him. He was about ten metres away. But the armed men remained silent and determined as they shifted their human cargo. They were apparently oblivious to Da Silva or any other witness. They didn't even look around to see if they were being watched. When they had accomplished their task — it took only seconds — they sped off in the ambulance, the white van following behind.

Da Silva, dazed and shaking, drove up to the gates of the Diniz household and sounded the alarm to Diniz's staff that their boss had become Brazil's latest kidnapping victim.

Inside the darkened rear section of the speeding ambulance, Abílio Diniz was thrown roughly to the floor, his head striking the metal surface, making him groggy. He battled to stay conscious. He was vaguely aware that his wrists and ankles were being bound and that a blindfold was tied around his head. He was relieved of his gun.

The ride was a short one. Within what seemed to him a matter of minutes, he was hauled from the vehicle and dragged into yet another vehicle, which felt similar to the first, a small sort of van or truck. This ride lasted a bit longer, and when it, too, ended, the precious, although beaten, cargo — a man with an estimated personal worth of U.S.$180 million — was dragged through passages and down steep, ladder-style stairs to the wooden box where the high-volume country-and-western beat was awaiting his arrival. As he landed on the floor of his cell with a thud, it occurred to Abílio that he had not heard his captors utter a word. Every move had been executed in disciplined silence.

Less than thirty minutes after Armando Da Silva had taken the news of the abduction to the Diniz family and prompted their call to the police, their phone rang. Abílio Diniz's sister, Vera, took the call. The message, spoken by a woman whose Portuguese was described as perfect, and without any trace of a foreign accent, told the family not to contact the police if they hoped for the safe return of Abílio.

The kidnappers told Vera that the negotiations for Abílio's freedom could be handled like any other high-level corporate deal. The woman kidnapper suggested that Luis Carlos Bresser Pereira, a board member at Pão de Açucar, should represent the family in their negotiations.

But the call for the family's silence came too late. The police were already at work. Witnesses were being rounded up, and a search of the area had begun by the time the kidnappers called. Not only had the police been informed, but Alcides Diniz, Abílio's brother, had also made a call to a British investigations and security firm that had carved out a niche for itself in Brazil by advising the families of kidnap victims on strategies for a safe release. The rich of Brazil did not have much faith in the abilities of the local police to bring a safe and peaceful end to a kidnapping. To appease the kidnappers, the telephone conversation ended with the family agreeing to bring in Luis Carlos Bresser Pereira, the kidnappers' preferred candidate for the job of negotiator, as requested. The initial ransom figure given to the family by the woman on the phone was U.S.$30 million.

Despite other high-profile kidnappings that plagued Brazil throughout the late 1980s, the Diniz kidnapping and subsequent massive ransom demand raised fears and eyebrows at all levels of Brazilian society. The news of the abduction moved quickly from the Diniz family home to corporate headquarters, to police forces, and, within hours, to the press. The consensus was that the boldness of the abductors showed clearly that they were serious and that they had been shrewd in their ransom demand, basing it on the family's ability to pay. The Diniz ransom would be a stretch, but if any family in Brazil could come up with that kind of money, it was this one, headed by seventy-five-year-old Portuguese immigrant Valentin Diniz, the patriarch.

The senior, ailing Diniz stepped back into the family business that afternoon, as soon as news hit the floor of the stock exchange that Abílio had been kidnapped. His steady hand, and the strong sense of business that had taken him from one small grocery shop in 1948 to a multinational organization and multibillion-dollar profits in the 1980s, would now steer his family and his company through crisis.

Fears that a gang of kidnappers was systematically targeting Brazil's wealthy grew when investigators noted similarities between Abílio's disappearance and that of Luiz Salles. Salles, too, was snatched in broad daylight, thrown in the back of a truck, and driven off. The Salles ransom was also considered to be within the bounds of what his family could afford. Authorities concluded that, if the same group was responsible, they were doing their homework, researching their targets and carefully choosing a ransom that was within reach.

As the family panicked, police scrambled, and stock brokers surveyed their potential losses, Abílio Diniz, his book unlaunched, sat huddled in a corner of his noisy cell.

CHAPTER 10

HUNTED

THE SÃO PAULO CIVIL POLICE'S GRUPO ANTI-SEQUESTRO (GAS), or anti-kidnapping team, was mobilized immediately when the abduction was reported. It wasted no time in coming up with the first significant piece of evidence — the white ambulance that just three hours before had carried Abílio from freedom into captivity. The kidnappers had not bothered to hide the vehicle, which was not, in fact, a real ambulance but a van with white-painted cardboard covering the windows, large red crosses on the sides, and a flashing red light mounted on the roof. The fake ambulance had been abandoned just twenty minutes after the kidnapping, steps from the home of Jãnio Quadros, who had been Brazil's president in 1960. The security guards at the home of the former president saw two men jump from the ambulance into a waiting white Opel van. The carelessness with which the van was disposed of led police to believe that the kidnappers were confident, even brazen, professionals. Whoever they were, they were certain they had left the van "clean," without any trace of its most recent occupants. Their confidence would cost them dearly.

Auto mechanics in São Paulo often leave their calling cards on the passenger-side dashboard of the vehicles they work on. The cards come complete with a notation indicating the date of the last repair, to help the owner keep track of the car's maintenance needs. The ambulance-van needed maintenance like any other vehicle. A thorough search by the police included the removal of the dashboard. When a vacuum cleaner was run along the gap behind it, a garage card was found. It had slipped through the paper-thin space between the dashboard and windshield, and it is unlikely that the van's occupants ever knew it was there.

The card led police to Auto Eletrico, located on Rúa da Consolacao, and to mechanic Cesar dos Reis Simplicio. He told them that the van had been brought in for work twice in recent weeks, the second time, four days prior to the kidnapping, for transmission and carburettor repairs. For the first round of repairs, a man described as middle-aged, with black hair and glasses, and speaking fluent Spanish, brought in the minivan. The second time, another man, described as younger, with glasses, had joined the original one.

As the hours passed, and Abílio Diniz's family and four grown children waited for his kidnappers to resume negotiations, police stood by with growing frustration while employees at the garage searched through their scraps of paper and invoices for an address, name, or phone number for the van's owners. The garbage had been collected three times since the van was picked up, the mechanics explained, and it was quite likely that the phone number had been thrown away. But, for the second time in as many days, luck seemed to be on the side of the investigators. Early on December 12, the day after Diniz was snatched, a phone number was found by garage employees and passed to police. They promptly tapped the line and waited for someone to call.

When no one called the number for several hours, police captain

Roberto Kauai, a senior member on the anti-kidnapping squad, grew impatient. He, along with another officer, went to stake out the Eldorado Hotel Apartments on São Paulo's Aureliano Coutinho, the address that corresponded with the phone number. A porter at the hotel told the officers that the man who had rented the apartment, Pedro Segundo Solar Venegas, had already checked out. Kauai, a twenty-two-year veteran of the force, asked the porter to call the station if the man returned. Two days after the number had been traced to the apartment, the excited porter called Kauai at 11:00 a.m. to say the man had come back and asked to get into the apartment, claiming he had left something behind. Kauai, along with Helenio Dell-Orso Prado and two other officers, raced back to the building and waited on the ground floor for the elevator to be called to the man's sixth-floor apartment. When the elevator stopped at the sixth floor, then returned to ground level, and the door opened, Kauai and Prado grabbed the occupant.

His real name was Ulisses Fernando Gallardo Acevedo, a Chilean who had rented the apartment under the false name of Venegas. When cornered by the two officers, Acevedo punched Captain Kauai in the face, knocking out two of his teeth in a futile bid at escape. Kauai, a judo expert and second-generation Japanese immigrant to Brazil, easily subdued the struggling man, who was taken back inside the apartment for five hours of questioning before he was transferred to police headquarters.

Acevedo's panicked reaction had perhaps been justified. The police, under mounting pressure to locate Diniz as they entered the fourth day of his kidnapping, beat their prisoner in the course of their interrogation. When he could take no more, Ulisses Acevedo confessed his role in the kidnapping. It turned out that he was the dark-haired man in sunglasses on the street corner who had identified the Mercedes and given the nod to other conspirators just four days earlier. That nod told his fellow kidnappers that their target was driving his white Mercedes, not the blue, two-door sports version that Abílio also owned, and that he was on his way to work. Ulisses Acevedo told police he did not know where the victim was being held. For security reasons, the group did not give any one individual all the details. He told police that only "Juan" and "Rubia" could lead them to Abílio Diniz. A search of Acevedo and his apartment turned up an electric bill for another apartment in the city's Higienopolis district, on Rúa Charles Darwin, and police set up their second stake-out in as many days outside the flat rented by a man using the name Juan Carlos Chariano.

On the morning of Friday, December 15, police were contemplating storming the apartment. They had taken over the apartment next door and now knew that the people inside were speaking Spanish. Kauai said he decided against trying to burst in in case they had a chain-lock on the door, which would slow officers down. If Abílio Diniz was being held inside that apartment, the delay might give his captors enough time to kill him. It was a risk the police could not take. So they waited. When a man and a woman left the apartment, they were followed into the elevator by two police officers, posing as a couple. The man even held the elevator door for the police. When the elevator doors reopened on the main floor, the officers decided that there were too many people around to risk making an arrest. Instead, they waited until the suspects were about to get into a Fiat Premio. At that moment, police swooped down and made the arrest.

Both fiercely resisted capture. The woman, Rubia, almost broke away from the female police officer who was trying to handcuff her. But a cop known as Petisco, or Munchie, a third-degree judo black belt, subdued both Rubia and her companion. He turned out to be Juan, the man who had rented the apartment. A short while later, two other men left the apartment and were arrested after another struggle. One of these men was Chilean Sergio Urtubia, the one-time Canadian resident believed to have crossed paths with Christine and David in Vancouver. The other man was Pedro

Lembach, another Chilean. The four joined Ulisses Acevedo at police headquarters, where they were turned over to the same interrogators who had beaten answers out of their colleague.

Police at the scene of the arrest combed the Fiat and the apartment for clues. They didn't have to look very hard to come up with countless pieces of evidence that tied the group directly, not only to the Diniz kidnapping, but also to the abduction four months earlier of Luiz Salles. They even found a tent which Salles told them was identical to the one in which he had been held prisoner during his ordeal. But the most damning piece of evidence was found in the purse of the arrested woman. Maria Emilia Honoria Marchi Badilla, code-named "Rubia," had written a new ransom note to the Diniz family negotiator, Luis Carlos Bresser Pereira, demanding that talks be sped up, and saying that the kidnappers were growing frustrated and wanted their money immediately. The note warned the family to call off the police and the media or else Abílio would be killed. Other evidence uncovered at the apartment included the Letraset used to create the phony ambulance decals and other false documents and a rubber stamp of the false name used by one of the two men arrested at the apartment on Rúa Charles Darwin. But the search did not produce the whereabouts of Abílio Diniz. For that information, police once again resorted to intimidation and torture.

By this point the disappearance was five days old. Police began to worry that the trail would go cold when news reached the other gang members that arrests had been made. If the victim was moved, then no amount of torture of the five already in custody would reveal his location. Or worse, the remaining gang members might panic, kill Abílio, and flee.

The case was not without its bizarre elements. It happened that the abduction and initial arrests fell during the final days of campaigning for Brazil's presidential election, the first such free and democratic election in twenty-nine years, and this circumstance proved to be significant. There had been a history of kidnappings

TOM HANSON / CANAPRESS

Christine's mother, Marilyn, takes her fight for her daughter's freedom to Parliament Hill during a rally in February, 1993.

ELENA VETTORAZZO / AGENCIA FOLHAS

ABOVE: *A weary Abílio Diniz stares out of the bathroom window of the kidnap house in São Paulo on the first day of the siege. He is flanked by brothers Horacio (right) and Humberto Paz.*

BELOW: *Hundreds of armed police surround the house as the siege enters its second day.*

CANAPRESS

ANTONIO GAUDERIO / AGENCIA FOLHAS

Archbishop Arns passes a note to the kidnappers during the final negotiations to free Abílio Diniz.

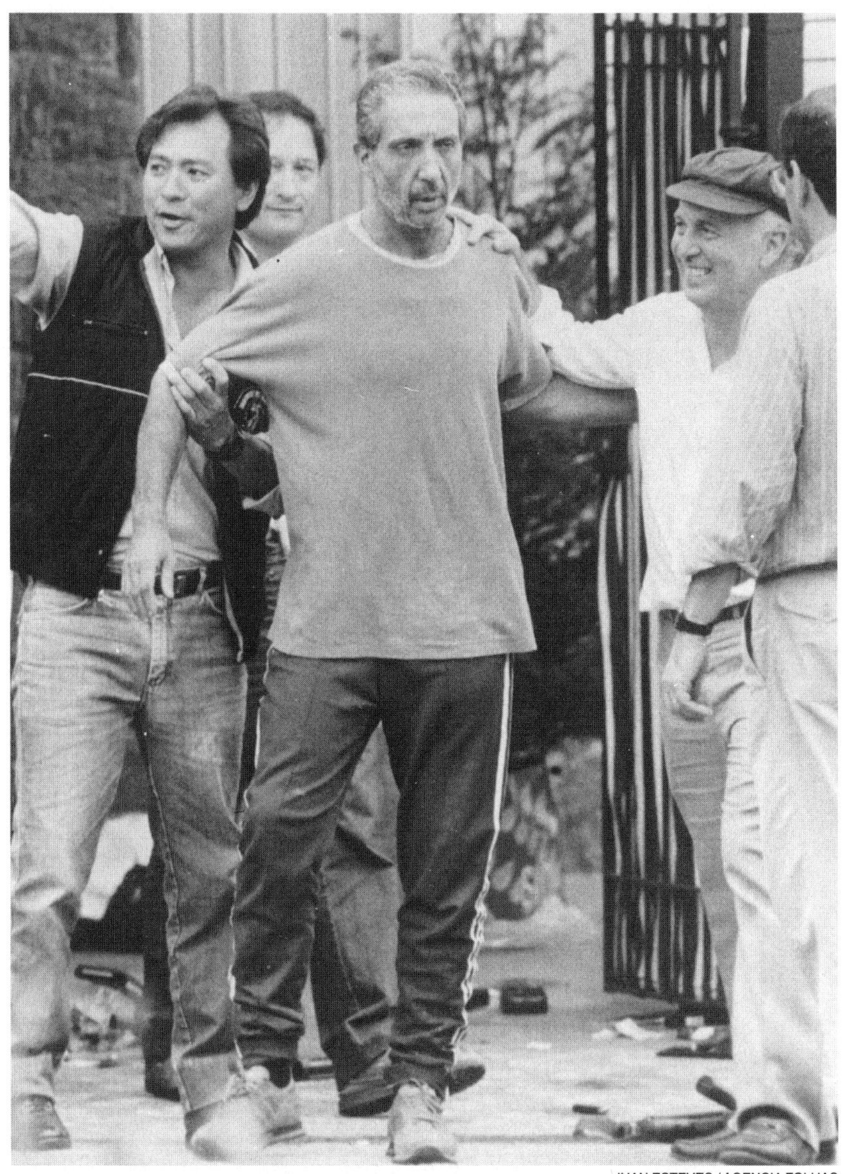

JUAN ESTEVES / AGENCIA FOLHAS

After six harrowing days as a hostage, Abílio Diniz stumbles to freedom. He is greeted by his friend and colleague, Luis Antonio Bresser Pereira, who took part in the negotiations.

JUAN ESTEVES / AGENCIA FOLHAS

ABOVE: *Christine is the first of the kidnappers to leave the house on Praca Hachiro Miyazaki.*

BELOW: *Next out of the house is David.*

JUAN ESTEVES / AGENCIA FOLHAS

Christine and David are exhibited before the Brazilian media in the São Paulo police station hours after their arrest.

CANAPRESS

MARCELO ZOCCHIO / AGENCIA FOLHAS

All ten kidnap suspects appear at a news conference. Some show the effects of police beatings.

CAROLINE MALLAN, JEAN-MARC BOUJU, RUBEN FARINA

A sampling of the more than two hundred documents discovered in the Nicaragua arms cache in May, 1993.

JEFF VINNICK

Marilyn and Keith Lamont, together with their daughters Elizabeth and Heather, look through the photographs of the documents uncovered in Nicaragua.

in Brazil, but, until this time, they were almost exclusively political in nature. The victims were mostly foreign diplomats, among them the West German and American ambassadors, who had been exchanged for left-wing political prisoners. The perpetrators had been leftists protesting the military regime that ran the country from 1964 until 1985, when civilian president José Sarney was installed. But, four years later, the election was under way again, and Alcides Diniz, Abílio's brother, was said by friends to be considering entering politics. Alcides was the youngest of the six children, and one of several relatives who had been ousted from the family business by Abílio the previous year. And he lit a fire under authorities when he wondered aloud to the Brazilian media if the bold abduction of his older brother, a model capitalist, might not have been the work of the now-legal socialist Workers' Party, which was in contention to rule the country after the final vote just days away.

In a move no doubt aimed at securing favours if right-wing candidate Fernando Collor de Mello, a close friend of Alcides Diniz, won the presidency, police said when they arrested Ulisses Acevedo that he was carrying stacks of Workers' Party literature. And then two of the five who had been captured, Ulisses Acevedo and Pedro Alejandro Fernandez Lembach, were paraded wearing green t-shirts with the logo of the Workers' Party or Partido dos Trabalhadores (PT), before the horde of Brazilian press photographers and reporters at an impromptu press conference held to update the Diniz case.

Footage from the press conference shows the exhausted men in tidy new t-shirts. Reporters in the media room on that day say they did not believe for a minute that the two men had been arrested wearing those t-shirts. But, given the history of kidnappings by Brazil's extreme left, the idea that some members of the PT might have been involved in snatching Diniz was not altogether farfetched. The reporters went with the story, and every major newspaper in the country ran blaring headlines suggesting that a connection had been established between Abílio Diniz's abductors and the PT, which was led by former union organizer Luis Ignacio de Silva, known throughout Brazil as "Lula." Lula had risen from former prisoner for his anti-government stand to Marxist congressman, before seeking the presidency.

As political games were played out in the media and election coverage ran a distant second to the Diniz case in every newspaper and on every television station in Brazil, the victim's family began to doubt they would ever see Abílio alive again. Abílio's wife, Auriluce, from whom he had been separated for three years, huddled in the family home with her four children and two young granddaughters, waiting for news. Their own investigators had come up with nothing. The people handling the ransom negotiations for the kidnappers had apparently been caught, so the family's negotiator was not receiving information about Abílio's condition. Police told the family that they had discovered medical supplies, including anaesthesia, surgical equipment, and antibiotics, which they took to be evidence of a plan to torture Abílio, perhaps cut off a finger or an ear to send to family in order to increase the pressure on them to come up with the $30 million. The family also feared, as the police did, that the remaining kidnappers would panic and kill their hostage when they learned of the arrest of their co-conspirators. The investigation seemed to be slipping out of control, and chaos to be taking over.

Political interference at every level of Brazilian government had turned an already dangerous situation into a deadly race to find Abílio Diniz. The Diniz family demanded that the case be turned over to the most experienced, trustworthy police officer with an expertise in terrorism.

CHAPTER 11

A CHANGE IN PLANS

THE TENSION INSIDE THE DINIZ HOME ON RUA SABUJI WAS equalled in the corridors of the São Paulo Civil Police headquarters. In response to the pressure exerted by the Diniz family, high-ranking investigators from the federal police force arrived in a flourish to reinstate order. They reorganized the investigating unit, selecting only the most respected local police officers to stay with the case.

The federal police in Brazil were led by a man known to most Brazilians as "The Sheriff." Romeu Tuma, the fifty-eight-year-old head of the federal force, had led several high-profile investigations. It was this small, round man who had announced to the world in 1985 that the body of a man who drowned in 1979 had been dug up from a small cemetery in the south of Brazil. With great fanfare and flourish, Romeu Tuma declared that the body belonged to despised, long-sought Nazi war criminal Dr. Josef Mengele. Tuma's other achievements included the capture of several high-ranking Italian Mafia figures who were running drugs through

Brazil in the 1970s. From his headquarters in Brasilia, Tuma, never one to shy away from the spotlight himself, declared his son, Romeu, Jr., in charge of securing Abílio Diniz's release.

Whether the younger Tuma agreed with the decision to beat the five suspects who had been arrested is not known. But, on December 15, with some of the most powerful people in the nation demanding answers and time running out in the hunt for the victim, violence was the method used to find the missing man, who, just two weeks shy of his fifty-third birthday, was quickly being elevated to superstar status in the media.

It was the man who had been arrested with Maria Badilla (Rubia), the Argentinian Humberto Paz, known as Juan Carlos, who broke down at the sight of Rubia being tortured and told police he would lead them to the house where Diniz was being held. In the early morning hours of Saturday, December 16, Paz insisted that all five suspects be taken to the secret location. He told police he would not reveal Abílio's whereabouts unless he was certain his co-accused would be unharmed. He said he had to go personally to the secret location to tell the others inside not to fire their guns but to give up peacefully. Otherwise, he told police, the gang members inside, who were heavily armed, would opt for a shoot-out that would most likely end in the death of Abílio Diniz.

Consequently, a small army of local, state, and national police vehicles crept slowly through the predawn streets of São Paulo, following the car which carried Humberto Paz. One of the two police officers in the car with Paz must have been having delusions of grandeur. This inexperienced officer, perhaps imagining himself bursting onto the scene and personally freeing Abílio and thereby gaining instant status as a national hero and defender of righteousness, stepped on the gas, causing their car to pull away from the others. Tuma's choice of officers had been lacking, co-workers would say later.

The car screeched to a halt outside 149 Praca Hachiro Miyazaki, the house that Paz had pointed to. Paz, in handcuffs, was dragged to the door by the would-be hero and his partner. The two policemen were caught completely off guard when the door flew open and the threesome found two machine-guns pointed at their heads. Paz was dragged inside. The São Paulo policemen, one of whom had fired a single shot in the seconds-long escape, were left standing outside the front door, lucky to be alive but minus their prized prisoner, when the back-up cars arrived seconds later.

When the realization hit that Paz had managed to slip past the thick wooden door to the house and through the fingers of an entire police force, mayhem erupted — both inside and outside the house.

Raimundo Rosélio Costa Freire had been awake and in the kitchen when Paz's warning came with a pounding fist on the door. Freire grabbed his gun, and along with one other man inside the house, took aim at the heads of the police officers standing beside Paz, their guns drawn and ready to fire. The gang members grabbed their leader, but not before his head had been grazed by a hastily fired bullet, and they slammed the door shut in the panicked faces of São Paulo's finest. Following orders amid the chaos, Freire ran through the kitchen at the rear of the house, through a small wooden door and down a wooden ladder. The blaring music did not distract him from his task. In fact, he had become used to it over the past five days. Freire had his handgun drawn as he slid back the bolt on the wooden door and yelled at Abílio Diniz to get up.

Abílio, weakened by the days spent lying in the two-foot by six-foot cubicle with the constant blaring music, could barely struggle to his feet. The light from beyond the open doorway was blinding after the almost total darkness of his captivity. Until that moment, virtually the only outside light had come from the peephole that had allowed his captors to watch him. The adrenalin in Raimundo Freire's voice told Abílio instantly that he was not being called upon because his release had been negotiated. Abílio, groggy and half awake, knew that the man who had delivered his meals without ever uttering a word was scared. Something had gone wrong.

Freire, speaking Portuguese, ordered Abílio out of the room at gunpoint. The prisoner tripped first over the small portable toilet, then the bottled water and the remains of a meal that lay on the floor. He was shoved through the door, then through an adjacent cubicle, where his guard was meant to sleep, and then on to the ladder. Abílio stumbled again as he tried to mount the sturdy wooden steps, but Freire pushed him upwards. Abílio emerged into a tiny, indoor, courtyard-like kitchen at the rear of a house. Abílio could hear the panicked yells of his captors as they raced around the house, throwing furniture up against the front door and windows. They spoke mainly Spanish, and one man's deep voice bellowed orders at the others, which Abílio understood. Abílio was led to the upstairs hallway, one of the few parts of the house without windows. It was as he was forcing his weakened legs up the stairs that he heard English being spoken for the first time. As he tried to focus on what was happening around him, he saw that his captors all carried guns, including Uzis, rifles, and shotguns. He was pushed to the floor, and his hands were bound again. He was told not to move, as the kidnappers continued to organize themselves.

Abílio Diniz had seen only two of his captors since the moment he was thrown into the back of the ambulance-van and blindfolded. One was Raimundo Freire, the other the Argentinian Hector Ramón Collante Tapia. Freire had not spoken to Abílio, but had only passed him notes in his cell and a flashlight to read them by. The notes had not given Abílio cause for optimism. They updated him on the state of negotiations, saying things were not going as smoothly or as quickly as they had hoped, and told him what to say in letters he was forced to write to his family, telling them to comply with his kidnappers' request for money and putting pressure on the family's negotiator. Each time the door had been opened and Raimundo Freire had passed him another note, it had included a reminder that his kidnappers were not afraid to kill him. One such note told Abílio that they had already built him a wooden coffin in case they needed to dispose of his body. Another of the notes read like a survey of his life. He was questioned at length about his family members, about details of the woman he had been dating for the past three months, whether he kept any other mistresses, or whether he took any regular medication. He was forced to give his captors a complete description of his twenty-five-year-old daughter, Adriana, and her daily routine, an exercise that sent chills of fear down his spine that displaced any worries he had about his own safety.

Hector Tapia, the other captor he had seen, had delivered food to his cell, always in silence. Despite the lack of direct communication during his five days underground, Abílio had managed to guess a bit about the nature of his captors. He suspected, for example, that some of them were foreigners. The food he had been given was made with good-quality meat, and some of the ingredients were very expensive, even in the estimation of the owner of Pão de Açucar. He did not presume that they had gone to this effort to satisfy his appetite, but rather that they themselves were used to food that was more elaborate than the simple Brazilian staples of rice and beans.

Now, sitting on the floor in the windowless hall, his sight returning after the initial shock of brightness, Abílio Diniz took stock of the people who had kept him prisoner for five days in the box where he thought he would die. It was obvious that most of them had been awakened from their sleep by the commotion. There was the silent man who had brought him some of his meals, his note-passing guard, another familiar-looking man who was now speaking Spanish to the big man — the one who had been issuing the orders moments ago — who looked as though he had been battered, and wore sweaty, torn clothing. Abílio guessed that it was the arrival of the battered man that had set off this frenzy. There was the girl, her hair a mess, her skin pale, her glance furtive, and her t-shirt and pants rumpled. And there was the small, intense-looking man with glasses, who also looked as though he had just jumped from his bed. He was trying to pry the handcuffs off the big man's wrists. These were the two, Abílio concluded, whom he had heard speaking English. He remembers thinking to himself for brief seconds that Americans were the last thing he expected to see when he finally came face to face with his captors. A civility that he credited to the Americans, comparable to that assumed of the British, made this pair's presence in the house, with guns drawn amid rising hysteria, seem wrong.

Once mattresses had been placed across windows and doors and other bits of furniture used to turn the house into a fortress, an eerie calm settled over all. Abílio soon recognized the big man, Humberto Paz, whom the others called "Juan," as the man who had worn a policeman's uniform just days earlier when he had yanked open the door of the Mercedes and struck Abílio the first few blows. This man, Paz, now announced that some of the "others" had been taken by police. He reassured them that they shouldn't worry, that their compatriots were outside in police cars and that he had insisted that they come along, and they would soon all be reunited. Although everything was definitely not going according to plan, all was certainly not lost. Paz went on to say that, despite the police outside, they were in a good position: they had the best bargaining chip of all. With these words, Paz nodded towards Abílio Diniz. The others all followed his glance.

Despite Paz's reassurances, his captors grew visibly uneasy as they became aware that the frenzy inside the house was matched by equally frenzied activity outside. They could hear the sounds of running footsteps at the side of the house, sirens in the distance, glass being smashed, and police officers yelling to each other in Portuguese.

Paz, eager to warn off any attack, crawled into the upstairs bathroom, placed his long-barrelled rifle between a crack in the shutters, and took aim through the window. His warning shot at police to keep back was answered with automatic gunfire that almost nicked his head again. The police sharpshooters were already in place and were not letting any opportunity pass them by. Paz was sent reeling back onto the bathroom floor in his sudden effort to avoid being hit. As he crawled back to where the others sat huddled in silence, Abílio Diniz among them, he told them again that it was just a matter of time until their escape was arranged.

As he spoke, someone on a loud-hailer could be heard calling to the *sequestros* (kidnappers) to give themselves up or die.

Negotiations for the life of Abílio Diniz were officially under way.

CHAPTER 12

HOLLYWOOD DREAMS

THE SHERIFF'S PRODIGY WAS ON THE SCENE. ROMEU TUMA, JR., the son of Brazil's legendary "supercop" and a federal police agent in São Paulo, was now in position to deal with the kidnappers. Tuma was willing to say just about anything to secure Abílio Diniz's freedom. But, from the very start, he was under orders from his father that the police would give these people nothing.

When Humberto Paz returned to the bathroom window to yell out to police, his voice displayed the same steely determination that ran through Romeu Tuma and had been passed from father to son.

From below the window, a bleeding Paz yelled to police that Abílio was with them and any attempt to storm the house would result in his certain death. Tuma demanded to know that Abílio had not been killed already. Paz turned and signalled for Abílio to be brought to the window. His Portuguese guard, along with the slight man with the glasses, the man Abílio Diniz thought was an American, dragged him into the bathroom. Police at the scene held their breath as the unshaven man with hollowed cheeks stared blankly through the small, horizontal panes of glass. A pistol was visible in the hands of an unknown captor, just off to the right of Abílio's head. Police now knew that the suspects were not bluffing. If Paz and company had not produced Abílio Diniz at that moment, officers who were at the house that day speculate that police would have stormed the house within minutes, shooting to kill as they went.

As the sun rose and the kidnappers sat in silence in the upstairs hallway, police on the other side of the front door mobilized for a full-scale assault. Reinforcements were called in, and the house surrounded. The next-door neighbours on both sides and to the rear of the house were evacuated, and police took over their homes. Sharpshooters patrolled neighbouring roofs. Three doors away, a command post was set up in the kitchen of Gertrudes Molina Rezador, who declined the offer of hotel accommodation and instead stayed in her home, making coffee for the growing assembly of police and family members. Abílio's family was notified. His brother, Alcides; family friend and negotiator Luis Carlos Bresser Pereira; another friend, Luis Fernando Sigaud Furquim de Campos, who sat on the board of directors at Pão de Açucar; and Abílio's twenty-six-year-old son, João Paulo, all arrived on the scene. The extent of the danger facing Abílio Diniz was not revealed to his wife and daughters, who remained cloistered in the family home under heavy guard. The four previously captured kidnappers, "Rubia," Ulisses Acevedo, Pedro Lembach, and Sergio Urtubia, who had been in cars that had followed Humberto Paz to the house, remained under heavy police guard and still sat handcuffed in the cars.

The police scrambled all around the house and neighbourhood for several hours, positioning themselves for an all-out assault. Throughout the period of waiting, Abílio Diniz watched as the woman in the house, whom he had heard called "Susanna," cleaned Paz's head wound. The leader then tried to rest on some blankets thrown down in the hallway. The others took turns guarding Abílio at gunpoint. They all remained very quiet, as though they thought that, by giving Paz the peace he needed to rest, he would be able to come up with a way to salvage their master plan. As the day dragged on, and Paz abandoned his attempts at fitful sleep, his much-anticipated plan began to take shape. Paz announced that they would demand cash, an armoured car, and an airplane fuelled and on the runway at the São Paulo airport in exchange for their prisoner. The release of the other members of the gang in police custody would also be demanded. The gang members nodded their heads in agreement. Abílio Diniz wondered to himself if he was the only one who saw the ludicrous idea for what it really was — a dream, and inspired by Hollywood no less. If that's what the others were thinking, however, their thoughts found no voice. In keeping with the discipline that had astounded Abílio throughout the siege, no one questioned the wisdom of Humberto Paz.

Noon approached, and Paz announced that the best way to secure the safety of everyone in the house while negotiations were going on was to have the media present. He scribbled a note that was thrown out the window, demanding that the media be summoned and complaining that he and the others arrested had been tortured. The note said police were not bargaining in good faith and blamed the state, the police, and the increasingly anxious family of Abílio Diniz for not striking a deal.

It seemed that it took only minutes before Paz's demand was met; hordes of media representatives arrived on the tiny street. When reporters learned that Abílio Diniz was inside the house, live television feeds were set up and satellite trucks brought in, and newspaper photographers and cameramen joined police sharpshooters on rooftops, all trying for the best possible shot. Some reporters and photographers got closer to the action than the police officers did. Claudio Julio Tognolli, a reporter with São Paulo's largest newspaper, *Folha de São Paulo*, arrived within minutes of the news of the siege hitting the newsroom. He quickly gained a position opposite the house, not only providing him with a vantage point but also placing him in sufficiently close proximity to overhear tidbits of conversation between the negotiators, as he waited for a deal to be struck. He was in for a long wait.

"It was the most tense, frightening scene I have ever witnessed," Tognolli recalls of the atmosphere that enveloped the run-down house. This mood of fear and tension was relayed to people across Brazil via live television coverage.

As Saturday passed without progress, news of the stand-off spread. As the final hours of presidential election campaigning were winding down, it seemed half of Brazil was glued to television sets to watch the Diniz drama unfold. From Brazilian cabinet ministers' offices all the way down to the police perched atop the roof adjacent to the house on Praca Hachiro Miyazaki, the message to those negotiating the stand-off, led by Romeu Tuma, was clear — no concessions would be made to the kidnappers.

It was late afternoon by the time Paz appeared at the bathroom window once again to speak with negotiators. He did so accompanied by Abílio Diniz in an effort to deter police marksmen. Paz threw another written message to the police, seeking assurances that the four other kidnappers, whose car had been moved up the street, were well. The note, written in Spanish, read: "We demand the liberty of our companions, an armoured car, a plane for ten people to leave the country. We will only come out with liberty. We will die with Abílio." The note also requested U.S.$200,000 in cash.

A message from Maria Badilla, Pedro Lembach, Ulisses Acevedo, and Sergio Urtubia was then passed along to police. It read: "We believe it must be considered that the solution of this case has a national and international transcendence, bearing great political repercussions, and that we must avoid any shedding of blood since we aren't murderers and we're not interested in anyone dying, here or there."

Negotiators did not keep the kidnappers waiting for an answer to their demands for an armoured car, fuelled airplane, and cash. The reply, again in the form of a note, was short and to the point and delivered within minutes. It was a flat no.

In the house being used as the command post, Alcides Diniz and Luis Carlos Bresser Pereira, along with Tuma, discussed the possibility of releasing political prisoners in Brazilian jails in return for the release of Abílio. This idea was quickly set aside, however, when it was realized that this kidnapping was different from those that had plagued the country in past years. These kidnappers were after money, a great deal of it. João Paulo Diniz, Abílio's son, kept in touch with family by telephone from the command post, letting them know of any new developments.

A reporter in the house at one point overheard João Paulo saying the family had already made an offer to the kidnappers for Abílio's release, but it had been rejected. He would not say how much the family had agreed to pay before negotiations had fallen apart with the arrest of Humberto Paz and the four others. Later the family would deny having made any offers, and in fact insisted that they had not even received a specific ransom demand.

It was Abílio's friend and colleague Luis Fernando Sigaud Furquim de Campos who worked to quell the panic of the negotiators whenever things appeared to take a turn for the worse. Alcides said he was worried that the mighty police presence would cause the kidnappers to "freak out and kill Abílio." When Tuma reported that the kidnappers were well armed, João Paulo Diniz called to tell his family that police considered Abílio's prison to be "a very dangerous house, more than we ever thought."

Inside the house, the quiet was deafening. Abílio could not understand what they were waiting for, or hoping for. It was obvious that there was no chance of escape. He could only hope that they did not decide to kill him anyway to prove some sort of twisted point. Despite the fear that gripped him, Abílio took some small comfort in the knowledge that police had tracked these people down, preventing them from planning any future attack on his family, particularly his daughter Adriana, in whom they had shown so much interest. After the days in which he had been subjected to constant, blaring music, Abílio could barely tolerate the quiet.

As darkness descended, the kidnappers called out to the police negotiators that they wanted to suspend talks from 11:00 p.m. until 6:00 a.m. the next morning. But part of the police strategy to get Abílio released was to deprive his captors of sleep, to wear them down, both for negotiating purposes and in case storming the house became necessary. Explosives experts had already been called in and had assessed the possibility of blowing the sidewalls off the house in a rescue attempt. Tuma told the kidnappers that police would keep in touch by calling to them every half-hour all night for updates on Abílio. Police also set up four large floodlights, which they shone into the windows of the house, again with the intention of keeping the kidnappers awake.

Meanwhile, Abílio's captors devised a watch schedule so that they could take turns getting some rest. Abílio surveyed his captors one by one. First, he focused on the girl, who was taking her turn acting as his guard. As she checked her handgun, jamming the clip firmly into place, Abílio thought to himself that he had never before seen a woman who could handle a gun the way this one could. As she took to her guarding task, her jaw jutted out, her eyes narrowed, and she fíxed Abílio with a hostile gaze. Next, he sized up the skinny man with glasses, who, like the girl, looked totally out of place among these men. He had a steady gaze and a calmness about him that Abílio found frightening. He spoke quietly, but with determination in his voice, as though he was used to being listened to without having to raise his voice. He, too, carried his handgun with confidence. Paz, who Abílio knew only as Juan, turned over as he tried to get comfortable, despite his wounds. He was a massive man in both stature and presence, and had probably been a leader as far back as his schooldays. The other large man, whom Abílio guessed was somehow related to Paz, looked similar, but younger, and lacked Paz's air of authority. His guard, whom he had come to know by sight over the past week, was of average height and followed orders instantly. He moved about the small area restlessly with a machine-gun tucked under his arm, the strap slung over his right shoulder. His other guard was a shorter man, middle-aged, and with a pot belly, who looked more like somebody's working-class father than a kidnapper. But he, too, did exactly what he was told and possessed the discipline that was a hallmark of the group.

Abílio knew that with darkness would come an increased chance that there would be an attack on the house by police. If his captors realized this, they did not say so. They spoke very rarely, but Paz assured them once more before trying again for sleep that, by daybreak, Abílio's family would insist on a settlement and all would be well. Paz then relaxed into a position in which he could sleep, and within minutes he was snoring.

But the police were not about to let the kidnappers enjoy a restful night. The anti-kidnapping squad began the first of several attempts to simulate a sudden invasion of the house. In addition to the floodlights, they used loud-hailers to give the kidnappers the impression that there were men on the roof, that the windows and doors were being smashed in, that the end was near.

The kidnappers scrambled to their feet, convinced at first that the invasion was real and the end had indeed arrived. Raimundo Freire, the Brazilian guard nicknamed Beto, announced that the police were "going to enter, let's shoot to kill," and raised his Israeli-made Uzi submachine-gun — a gun capable of firing nine hundred rounds a minute — in readiness.

In what Abílio Diniz would later offer up as an example of the sort of discipline that prevailed inside the house, Humberto Paz called out to each kidnapper by name and asked three questions:

"Are you ready? Are you decided? Are you prepared?" He went through the questions as he called roll: "Modesto? Susanna? Maguila? Bebe? Hector?"

Each answered in a firm voice that he or she was ready to shoot to kill if that was what was necessary. As each one spoke, each raised his or her weapon to demonstrate preparedness. Through listening devices planted on the sidewalls of the house, police heard parts of conversations from the upstairs hallway. They heard this vow to kill and knew that the people they were dealing with had both the training and the military-like discipline to honour their vows.

The fake invasion was successful in that it kept the kidnappers awake for most of the night, although Abílio was surprised to see that they did seem to be able to take short naps, despite the noise. Abílio wondered if each had begun to think that surrender was the most likely outcome. As they tired, they began to talk. Abílio was told that the reason he had been subjected to the loud music was as a means of subduing him should he offer any resistance. The mental fatigue caused by the music made him easier to handle, and more willing to answer their questions and write the notes. The men talked of the huge chasm between rich and poor in Brazil, and they told their victim that the money from his abduction would help right the wrongs South America's ruling class had perpetrated on the impoverished majority. Abílio agreed with much of what they had to say and was surprised at their level of education. He realized that he had not been the chance victim of a band of hoodlums looking to make some fast money, but rather a pawn in a calculated, deadly game played by people who knew very well how to win. These people were not alone in this act of terrorism; they were part of something much larger. Abílio overheard them discussing the various investments they would make with the money from the kidnappings they had planned. He would later refer to his captors as "very cultured."

It was during this early-morning talk that Abílio tried to speak

English to the girl, Susanna, and the skinny, small man, who they called "Modesto" (the modest one), who had continuously urged calm among his fellow kidnappers. Abílio asked in English what they were doing with this organization, but Modesto just turned and looked at him, an annoyed expression on his face, as though he had not expected his prisoner to speak English. He turned away without answering. Abílio did not hear English spoken again. When Paz finally spoke to the victim, Abílio realized that the leader's one true fear was torture at the hands of police. It was obvious the man had already been badly beaten, and police brutality was well documented in Brazil. But, Abílio wondered to himself, if the situation were different would Paz resort to torture to find out what he wanted to know? To get his way? He had already resorted to kidnapping, and Abílio was left with the impression that he was not the only one on the gang's list of victims, past or future. Was the mind-numbing music not a form of torture? What were the group's plans for his young Adriana, in whom they had expressed so much interest? Paz told him he had already been tortured by police three times in his life and had been imprisoned while still a teenager for speaking his mind. Abílio, his wrists and ankles still swollen from the chicken wire that this very man had used to bind him, found himself sympathetic nonetheless. Humberto Paz, despite his threatening six-foot, four-inch frame, his deep stare, and his deftness with a weapon, was a very convincing man.

The group huddled together in the hallway through much of the night as the mock-invasion continued. By daybreak, the discussion, led mainly by Humberto Paz, convinced the kidnappers, now weary, dirty, and thirsty, to accept the reality that they must surrender to get out of the house alive. Abílio Diniz let out a sigh of relief that the gang had abandoned the idea of a high-flying getaway, armoured car and all. At daybreak on Sunday, December 17, 1989, voting day in Brazil, negotiations for the release of one of Brazil's wealthiest men finally began in earnest.

CHAPTER 13

CANADIANS?

ALCIDES DINIZ AND LUIS CARLOS BRESSER PEREIRA HAD SPENT the night at the kitchen table in the neighbour's house just steps away, drinking black coffee and trying to come up with a deal that would satisfy the kidnappers and free Abílio. They were huddled with police negotiators, family friends, and representatives of the investigations firm from Britain who were there to offer advice, when the call came from the bathroom window. The negotiating team scrambled for a better position to hear what Humberto Paz had to say this time. The events of the previous day had not left Alcides in an optimistic mood. The outrageous getaway demands of the kidnappers were beyond comprehension. These people had been caught: there was no way they were going to be handed their freedom, let alone given the use of a fuelled airplane. The mock invasion of the night before had, in addition, left Alcides Diniz wondering if his brother's life was still there to negotiate for. Had the kidnappers panicked and killed their captive? Would he have to tell his nieces and nephews that they no longer had a father? What would he say to his own father?

Just after dawn, in answer to Humberto Paz's summons, Luis Carlos Bresser Pereira climbed onto the roof of the garage adjoining the side of the house. The terrorist leader was asking for assurances that surrender would not mean death or torture of any of the accused. He wanted a guarantee that there would be a fair trial, without police interference.

Alcides Diniz, after discussions with Luis Carlos Bresser Pereira, dispatched a message to the Archbishop of São Paulo, Dom Paulo Evaristo Cardinal Arns, asking for his assistance in negotiating the surrender. Arns was one of the most politically active clergymen in Brazil, well known for his activism on behalf of human rights. He was aboard a Diniz family helicopter on his way to the kidnap house within the hour. The helicopter landed in the tiny parkette across the street from the kidnap house, and television crews followed him as he ran towards it.

The sixty-eight-year-old Arns climbed a ladder beside the garage to reach the bathroom window and talk to Humberto Paz. Paz repeated to the priest his message that there had to be a fair trial and no more torture. Arns, moving between the police and family negotiators, the victim's brother and Paz, spent hours hammering out a deal for surrender. Abílio remembers that during the negotiations someone made coffee and offered him some, but he had no stomach for it. He was not entirely convinced that his captors were sincere in their offer to surrender. He sensed that they thought it would be impossible to get a fair trial and spoke up, offering to pay their legal fees if they gave themselves up. He told them that he understood the motives behind their actions, and knew their fears of torture were legitimate. He offered to spend whatever it took to ensure that they had reliable legal counsel to help them fight the kidnapping charges. At first Paz was taken aback by Abílio's suggestion. But, after almost thirty hours in the hallway of this rundown house, Abílio felt he had very little to lose. The money was not an issue for him, and anything that would speed up a possible release was worth the attempt.

Paz quizzed him as to why he would make such an offer. What guarantees could he give that he wouldn't pay off the lawyers to keep them behind bars? Paz asked. Abílio, weak and tired after more than thirty-six hours without food, could offer nothing more than his word. He told Humberto Paz that he would give his word on the defence fees in return for the gang leader's word that he or any other member of his family would not be harmed. Paz looked at his haggard victim and nodded his head in agreement. He then summoned Arns once again to pass along the news that a deal had been arranged.

The next step for the kidnappers was to take precautions to ensure that they were not slaughtered as they tried to give themselves up. The media had provided a safety net, but still the kidnappers needed more concrete assurance than that offered by TV cameras. Paz passed a note to Arns, asking for the presence of Chilean, Argentine, and Canadian consular officials to witness the surrender. It was when he overheard this that Diniz realized for the first time that his English-speaking captors must be Canadians. He struggled through his haze of exhaustion to come up with a reason why Canadians would find themselves in this house, armed to the teeth, faces set in determination, vowing to fight to the death.

On the Sunday before Christmas, no one was answering the phone at the Canadian consulate in São Paulo. A message on the answering machine gave the home number of Consul General William (Bill) Ross. When police tried his house, Ross wasn't there either. Although he had caught some of the television coverage of the siege at the kidnap house the evening before, Canada's new consul general had not paid much attention. He was battling São Paulo's legendary traffic on this beautiful Sunday, as he made his way to the airport to pick up his wife and children, who were arriving from Canada for Christmas. Ross had only been in Brazil a few weeks himself, and his family had not made the move to join him yet.

As the negotiating team huddled outside the house under the afternoon sun and waited for news of the consular officials' arrival, they wondered about the woman who could be seen glancing out the bathroom window. She seemed to survey the crowd outside, before backing away from the window. They wondered, too, about the younger man with glasses who joined Humberto Paz at the window from time to time, always whispering into the ear of the leader as talks continued.

When the call had come for Canadian, Chilean, and Argentine officials, Romeu Tuma, Jr., also thought it strange that Canadians might somehow be involved. He guessed immediately that the woman was one of the Canadians among the gang.

From what he knew of Canadians, Tuma could not conceive of how this woman had come to be in Brazil, with a gun in her hand and Abílio Diniz under her guard. Was this not a country known for ice hockey, mountains, and peaceful, well-organized democracy?

In an upper-class São Paulo neighbourhood, the Canadian trade commissioner Pierre Pichette had caught glimpses of the stand-off on the evening news the night before. This morning, his young son was watching the television coverage of the siege. The scene unfolding included Archbishop Arns on his ladder, speaking with Humberto Paz, while other kidnappers glanced out the window from time to time. Abílio Diniz had also been brought to the window intermittently to reassure police that he was still alive and remind them that he could still serve as a shield, should they decide to bargain in bad faith. The Pichettes were aware of what was happening, but, with Christmas just days away and beautiful weather outside, they had not paid much attention. But when the younger Pichette heard a call over the television for a representative from the Canadian consulate to contact police immediately, he ran to tell his father. The trade specialist called São Paulo police immediately.

Pichette was told that the kidnappers had agreed to surrender but were demanding the presence of a representative from the Canadian government. Pichette told police he would have to call External Affairs headquarters in Canada and ask for permission to participate in the surrender. Permission was granted. Further attempts were made to locate Bill Ross, but, in the interim, Pichette, under police escort, made his way to Praca Hachiro Miyazaki.

Pichette was the last of the consular officials to arrive. It was after 1:00 p.m. when he joined the Argentine and Chilean representatives outside the house. Accompanied by the archbishop, the three men climbed onto the roof of the garage and leaned around the corner of the house to show the kidnappers their diplomatic identification.

Pichette introduced himself in Spanish to Paz, who inspected the identification Pichette was holding in his outstretched hand. Pichette had to strain to give the kidnapper a close look at the card. Paz told him to stay put: he had someone he wanted him to meet.

The skinny man, whom Abílio Diniz had come to know as Il Modesto, came to the window and calmly asked Pichette in English who he was and where he was from. After he had answered to the young man's satisfaction, Il Modesto said, "I'm Canadian. My name is Dave Spencer."

As David moved away from the window, the girl known as Susanna, with bags under her eyes, approached the window and told Pichette: "I'm Chris Lamont, from Langley, B.C."

"Up until that second I had no idea there were Canadians involved; no one ever even guessed it," Pichette said, recalling his surprise at finding the pair in the midst of the biggest story to hit Brazil in years. Pichette, along with other consular officials who would come to know David and Christine in the months ahead, were always struck by how calm David remained throughout the siege and subsequent trial and imprisonment.

"If I was in that house, I think David Spencer would be a good person to have in there; he was always so calm and in control, he would keep things cool," a consulate employee would later remember.

With verification of his credentials complete, Pichette and the other consular officials, along with Archbishop Arns, retreated. The deal they had struck gave the kidnappers until 4:00 p.m. to surrender. After that, the agreement expired. Both nerves and patience had been sorely tried for more than thirty-four-hours, but an end to the siege was finally in sight. Auriluce Diniz, Abílio's former wife, was caught by the television cameras as she stood outside the house with Alcides and wept openly for the fate of the father of her children.

When Pierre Pichette descended the ladder and told police that two of the kidnappers had claimed to be Canadian, Tuma and his colleagues began to view their adversaries in a different light. Did this gang of kidnappers extend outside of South America? The talks had been carried out in a mixture of Spanish and Portuguese, so police knew that South Americans from outside of Brazil were involved. But were they perhaps dealing with something larger? An organization that reached as far north as Canada? Who else was involved in this abduction, and where were they from? Had Abílio Diniz been just the first piece in a puzzle? The first sacrificial pawn in a reign of terror? How much more was to come? Who else was being targeted, perhaps at this exact moment?

Once the consular officials had disappeared from view, Humberto Paz turned away from the window and joined the others on the floor in the hallway. He told them he was confident that they would be well treated and assured of a fair trial. Abílio Diniz watched as they talked about the deal they had worked out. Then, one by one, they went into the bathroom and showered, and then changed into clean clothes. As the clock ticked towards four o'clock, each kidnapper emerged from the bathroom with wet hair and a clean look. The girl, Susanna, put on a skirt, and the men found white shirts. This was a gesture that Abílio Diniz would later call "vain and proud." To their victim's amazement, the six kidnappers then produced a bottle of red wine, and toasted the completion of a good deal with police. Abílio was invited to participate, but declined, saying he had not eaten in so long he didn't think he could possibly drink wine. At their insistence, he did raise an empty glass, however, and took part in the spirit of the toast. The group then put down their dirty kitchen cups and, one by one, stood up and very slowly headed down the stairs towards the front door.

Christine Lamont squeezed the hand of David Spencer and walked out of the house. She squinted into the late-afternoon sun and walked past the wrought-iron gate with a calm gaze, her hair still damp from her shower. She wore black flat shoes, black pantyhose, and a black skirt with a long-sleeved printed blouse tucked in. She kept her hands at her sides as she was quickly surrounded by police wearing bullet-proof vests. They searched her for weapons, handcuffed her, and ushered her onto a waiting bus just steps away. Christine was followed by David, who came out with his hands up. He was wearing a crisp white shirt and dark pants. He too was frisked and placed aboard the bus. One by one, the others followed. Humberto Paz was the last of the kidnappers to emerge, standing tall and smiling despite his wounds.

The three consular officials, along with Archbishop Arns and several of the police officers, also boarded the bus for the ride to the police station. After the excitement and commotion that attended the kidnappers' surrender, there was a pause, then Abílio Diniz stumbled out the front door of the house to the cheers and applause of the media and police officers. He looked disoriented as police surrounded him and reporters rushed to hear his words. Luis Carlos Bresser Pereira could be seen smiling, slapping his friend on the back. But this was not the same businessman who had been snatched from his Mercedes six days before. He was thinner and weaker, and wearing navy-blue jogging pants, a dirty grey t-shirt, and white running shoes. He seemed at a loss for words, and appeared to be on the verge of passing out.

"These were, without a doubt, the worst moments of my life, but it is all over now, it is all over," he mumbled before being whisked off for a reunion with his family.

Abílio went first to his former wife's house, where his children had gathered for his homecoming. Behind closed doors, the family fed Abílio cake and milk in a feeble attempt to restore him to his former robustness. But food could not erase the haunted look in the man's eyes as he hugged his family close to him and told them of the "cave" in which he had spent the last week, the cave that he was at times certain would also serve as his tomb.

While Brazilians rejoiced at the release of a financial celebrity and police officers jockeyed to take credit for a job well done, the images of a band of kidnappers walking out of the house with heads held high were broadcast across the country. Whereas the victim of this brutal drama seemed reduced in stature and so weak that he struggled to stay on his feet, the kidnappers looked dignified, almost proud. The upturned faces of the people who had done this would be remembered by Brazilians for years to come.

CHAPTER 14

WALL OF SILENCE

IN THE DAYS AFTER ABÍLIO STAGGERED FROM THE KIDNAP HOUSE, stories about the abduction took on a life of their own. Speculation swirled especially around the role of the Canadians. One newspaper reported that police sources were labelling David Spencer the strategist and Christine Lamont the provider of food and materiels in the operation. Another story suggested that the $2.5 million ransom from the earlier abduction of Luiz Salles had been smuggled into Canada for safe-keeping. Still other stories were published that questioned how two educated Canadians could have found themselves working with international terrorists.

Brazil's largest newspaper, *Folha de São Paulo*, asked the question on many people's minds: "What could motivate two university students from a country where the ultra-left is limited to walks for peace for human rights to take part in a political kidnapping?"

Although police in São Paulo found it hard to understand how the two Canadians came to be in the line of criminals emerging from the kidnap house, they did not offer any excuses for the couple. Both refused to give a statement to police during questioning, which only served to fuel the speculation about their roles in the abduction.

"One thing is certain: they were playing a dangerous game. They were on a course that could only end in one of two ways — kill or be killed," said Inspector Gilberto Cunha following the arrests. Cunha told reporters that a video cassette uncovered in an apartment rented by one of the kidnappers showed Christine and David in some kind of camp, performing military, combat-like exercises.

The disciplined silence that Abílio Diniz had observed during his captivity, that Pierre Pichette had observed during his time with the accused, and that the investigators had seen during questioning was to be carried through until the trial began. Whatever the Canadians were doing with these people, they weren't offering up any comment by way of a defence. They were waiting to "tell it to the judge." But exactly what it was they were prepared to tell the man who would decide their guilt or innocence remained a mystery.

Christine and David didn't have long to wait for their day in court. Just nineteen days after they surrendered to police and Abílio Diniz was freed live on national television, the trial of Brazil's notorious *sequestros* began amid much publicity and overwhelming security.

The motorcade that pulled out slowly from behind the walls of the São Paulo state prison complex included twelve police cars, led by four motorcycles. In the middle of the procession were two armoured cars, carrying the accused. Guards shouldering machine-guns surveyed the scene from the watchtower. Inside the armoured cars, the prisoners sat with wrists and ankles shackled.

As the motorcade made its way to the grey concrete courthouse in a run-down district of São Paulo, the dark outlines of sharpshooters in the bright early-morning sun could be seen on neighbouring roofs. Police officers wearing heavy bullet-proof vests patrolled around the courthouse with German shepherds, sweat pouring off them in the tropical summer sun. Those attending the trial, including staff from the Canadian consulate who were to monitor the proceedings, were searched as they entered the building. Inside, more rifle-toting police officers with dogs walked the corridors of the brightly lit building, scanning the crowd for anyone who looked out of place, even a little bit nervous. The bomb squad had already done a sweep of the building before prison officials were given the go-ahead to bring in the accused. Still, guards, outfitted with machine-guns, grenades, and tear-gas canisters, searched for any unattended packages or briefcases that might hide explosives.

When the motorcade came to a stop in front of the low-rise building, police lined the sidewalk as the prisoners were led inside. The police brass who had orchestrated this elaborate transfer breathed a silent sigh of relief when the prisoners were locked in their holding cells beside the courtroom. The level of security was not a matter of routine in São Paulo, nor was it guided by paranoia. Four days before the January 5 trial began, prosecutors had petitioned the courts to hold the trial itself inside the prison compound, so as not to risk having to transport the accused. Investigations in the days after Abílio Diniz was freed revealed that police were dealing with a much more sophisticated terrorist organization than they had first imagined. They also soon realized that, as sweeping as the ten arrests had been, there were probably as many as twenty others involved in the kidnapping. Members of the first, second, and third teams remained at large. The discovery of two Canadians among the company raised fears of an international kidnapping ring whose territory extended far beyond the bounds of South, or even Central, America. The type and quantity of arms found in the various houses and apartments rented by the kidnappers, including plastic explosives, led police to believe that those who remained free probably had the firepower to orchestrate a break-out. Odds were that they might even succeed, and spilled blood of Brazilian police or civilian bystanders would be of no concern to these people.

Police had learned a lot about the people they were dealing with in a relatively short time. What they found out did not lull anyone into thinking that this kidnapping was exceptional, an oddity that would never be repeated in Brazil. The evidence in the hands of the prosecution suggested what the police investigators already knew: if it had not been for sheer luck, the kidnapping of Abílio Diniz would have been just the first in a wave of cowardly crimes to be committed all over Brazil. Dossiers located in the apartments rented by the kidnappers contained chillingly precise details about the daily routines of more than thirty of Brazil's wealthiest citizens. The files included information about families, mistresses, squash-court bookings at health clubs, jogging routes, and favourite restaurants. The information had been neatly typed and photographed, the slides slipped under book jackets. In addition to the rich, the dossiers also contained details of the lifestyles of various high-ranking police officers in both the São Paulo and the federal police forces. The details were so accurate, complete with photographs of officers' young children, that some officers were forced to pack up their families and have them moved to safehouses until the trial was over. Some police officers moved permanently and took steps to cover their tracks, fearing that the kidnappers who remained at large would hunt them down. Investigators guessed that following the police officers had been part of a back-up plan to exchange hostages, most likely children, for those arrested if something went wrong in the Abílio Diniz kidnapping. Prisoners in cells near those of the accused reported hearing talk of plans to kidnap the judge's family for a prisoner exchange.

São Paulo's First Criminal Court was the domain of Judge Roberto Caldeira Barioni. Judge Barioni had originally ordered the trial to be closed to all but interested parties. Then, suddenly, the day before the trial was set to begin, he changed his mind and said the press would be allowed into the courtroom. With his original ruling that barred the press, Judge Barioni was trying to staunch some of the flood of publicity the case was receiving and allow those involved to conduct themselves in a professional manner. He hoped to control the high emotions of a public that was outraged by the audacity of these foreigners operating in Brazil. But, as screaming headlines in the press called for a return to death sentences for kidnappers, the judge rescinded his decision in order to keep the process as open as possible, and therefore above reproach and accusations of secrecy.

The Brazilian justice system operates like that of some European countries, such as Italy and Switzerland. The judge acts as both interrogator and jury. He personally questions the accused, the witnesses, and the victim before hearing oral submissions from both the prosecution and the defence attorneys. As the final step, written submissions are also made by the attorneys before a written judgement is handed down, usually within a matter of weeks. The judge's decision includes the sentences. He alone makes the final call. He decides who is lying and who is telling the truth, who is credible and who is making a mockery of the system. Brazilian law presumes guilt, not innocence, when the accused are caught "red-handed" in a crime, which was the case with the Diniz kidnappers.

Judge Barioni, a quiet, patient man, does not look like the hardliner he has sometimes been made out to be. He is soft-spoken and almost casual in the way he questions those who find themselves before him. He wears gold wire-rimmed glasses, nods his head frequently, and takes notes constantly without looking down at the notepaper. He gazes intently at the people he is questioning, as though he's hoping to see beyond their pat answers, to see who they really are, not who they claim to be. He pays particular attention to body language, nuances in the tone of voice, and the time it takes for a question to be answered. He has a track record of hearing high-profile cases with a serenity that belies the pressure surrounding them. He also does his homework. When he asks questions, he often already knows the answers. He does not speak quickly, or press his subject for fast responses, but rather gives the person testifying an opportunity to think about the question that has been asked. His extensive knowledge of the case is often concealed behind seemingly inane questions. But, in his years as a judge, Barioni discovered that this is a good tactic for getting at the truth. He lulls the person being questioned into thinking that the judge doesn't know about the case he is trying, that he can be lied to without risk. It's a tactic that has served Barioni well in getting at the truth.

Christine Lamont and David Spencer did not know about Barioni's tactic.

Their testimony before Judge Barioni was the first order of business on the first day of the trial once all the lawyers had introduced themselves to the judge. The accused were brought out to testify one at a time, the others remaining in holding cells.

Christine Lamont was the first to stand and be interrogated, using an interpreter. She wore a prison-issue khaki skirt that fell to just below her knees and a green knit short-sleeve top with beige trim around the neck. Her dark, straight hair hung limply at the sides of her pale face, and there were dark circles under her eyes. Christine already had the wrinkles of a chain smoker, and the deep lines around her mouth and eyes made her appear older than she was. Her stained teeth and messy hair gave her a rough edge, and her quiet voice had a gravelly tone from too many cigarettes. She stared at the floor and answered Judge Barioni's many questions in a voice that was barely more than a whisper. He noticed that this Canadian woman did not look him in the eye when she gave him answers. The answers themselves sounded to him as though they had been often and well rehearsed.

If there was ever a moment in the life of Chris Lamont to stand up straight, look a man in the eye, and tell the truth, it had just arrived. If she was, as she would later claim, a scared Canadian who had got in over her head with people capable of things she could not imagine, then the time had come to be a songbird — to tell her story — all of it, good and bad — from beginning to end.

If, as she later claimed, she did not even know that Abílio Diniz was being held captive in a cell under the house in which she was living, this was the proverbial moment of truth. It was time to let the others fend for themselves and be damned, if that's what it took to get the truth across. She had to come out of her interrogation looking sincere and innocent. Even if the truth was at times incriminating, it was her best hope of getting out of this mess. But Christine Lamont chose another path. She told Barioni a string of lies.

As her questioning began, Christine Lamont interrupted her translator to ask if she could tell her story.

"Yes, by all means," replied Barioni.

In 132 words and less than two minutes, Christine Lamont gave her edited version of how she and David Spencer came to be in a São Paulo house with one of Brazil's richest men staring down the barrel of a gun that had Christine's finger on the trigger.

"David and I met three and a half years ago. Last summer we decided to travel through Latin America. We left Canada in June from Vancouver and stayed in Mexico for two or three days, spent a few days in Panama, and then came here for more or less two weeks. Then, at the end of July, beginning of August, we went to Argentina and then returned here. At that time David went to the house at 149 Hachiro Miyazaki. Two days later we moved in; two men who are also accused moved into the house. During that time, David and I went out every day, and those men were usually asleep when we left the house. We shared the house with these men but very seldom talked to them. I only found out about the kidnapping the day the police arrived."

Lamont further testified that she didn't even know her roommates' names. Nor could she remember when she and David Spencer first moved into the house. She guessed that it was at the beginning of October 1989. She also said that she didn't know anything about a young foreign couple matching their description who had gone to the São Paulo water and electric department, asking for a copy of the plans for the street the house was on. The plan included details of wells no longer in use that had been dug under the houses. She said she did not even know that Abílio Diniz's cell existed until police had surrounded the house. Lamont testified that David had bought a white Volkswagen Kombi van but added that they rarely used it during the day. She said David was the only one who ever drove the Kombi.

To the very straightforward question, "Where were you on December eleventh?" Lamont replied: "What day of the week was that?" Judge Barioni, patient as always, told her it was a Monday, and Lamont replied: "I can't remember, we were usually looking for courses in Portuguese, shopping, or sight-seeing."

If Lamont's story was to believed, then Judge Barioni needed a straightforward answer to the next obvious question: "Why didn't you give yourself up when the police arrived at the house?"

"Two reasons. One, nobody asked me to come out, and the other, because the house was completely surrounded. If they had asked, I would have come out."

To these two reasons, Lamont later added that the person who had come to warn them of the police attack, Humberto Paz, had been tortured, and she was afraid. She told Barioni that she thought the only reason she was on trial was because she was living in that house. In a phrase that would be echoed for years to come, Chris Lamont said that essentially she and Spencer had been in the wrong place at the wrong time.

This denial of any wrongdoing brought the judge to his next round of questioning. Could Christine Lamont tell the court why she was carrying a passport that wasn't in her real name?

"When we were in Argentina we lost our papers and David gave me that one. . . . I didn't think I was doing anything wrong."

Christine went on to tell Judge Barioni that she knew nothing of a cache of medical supplies and drugs, including Valium and antibiotics, that was found in the house. Nor did she know anything about the twelve guns of varying origins and calibres found after the kidnapping ended. Aside from the two people she remembered as her former roommates, Christine said she did not know any of the other accused. She denied ever having met Raimundo Freire, the only Brazilian charged, and the man who acted as Abílio Diniz's guard during his six days in captivity. Given that Raimundo did not leave the house during Diniz's captivity, and brought the victim most of his meals, Barioni had a hard time believing that Christine had not even passed him in the kitchen of the home. Christine admitted to holding a gun during the siege, but said she hadn't even loaded it herself, adding that she wouldn't know how.

"You had a revolver?" Barioni asked.

"Yes," she replied.

"What for?"

"I had the impression that the police were going to invade the house and I wanted to protect my life and David's. And also Abílio."

But Abílio Diniz remembered Chris Lamont, not as his defender, but as his captor, taking her turn standing guard over him.

Christine said she didn't remember anyone in particular being in charge after police surrounded the house and the siege began. She also said she didn't remember when or why her co-accused started calling her "Susanna." She didn't remember whether or not she was there when David signed a lease for the kidnapping house. Christine also said she felt no ill-will towards the people who had landed her in prison, accused of a kidnapping she claimed to be innocent of, with a possible sentence of more than twenty years in jail ahead of her.

Barioni then ran slowly down a short list of addresses, four in total, asking if she was ever at any of the apartments mentioned.

Her reply was a prompt "No" to each address. Once again, Barioni scribbled a note to himself. Although the judge did not let on that he suspected anything was amiss, he wrote that Christine had denied any knowledge of the fourth and final address on the list, 295 Rúa Francisco Pugliesi. In fact, Judge Barioni had in his possession a photocopy of the six-month lease for the house on Rúa Francisco Pugliesi that was signed by Lisa Lynne Walker and Paul Joseph Gomes Mendes. It was dated August 17. Lamont had already told the judge that she and David Spencer were in Argentina at the time the lease clearly showed they were house shopping in São Paulo.

This was the house that Christine and David had hastily vacated, despite weeks worth of renovations, when they discovered that a policeman lived across the street.

Barioni could only shake his head after hearing Christine out. He was so obviously being lied to that he hardly knew whether or not to bother going on with the questions.

The passport in the name of Lisa Lynne Walker had been used by someone to enter Brazil in early July, more than a month before Lamont and Spencer say they were in Argentina. Christine testified that it was in Argentina that David gave her this fake passport, but the evidence before Barioni showed that she had had the document weeks before that trip.

It was clear that they had been using fake passports and assumed identities ever since they had arrived in Latin America and not, as they claimed, only after they had lost their real passports. The young lady before him was losing credibility about as quickly as Judge Barioni was losing his famed patience.

CHAPTER 15

MEMORY LAPSES

BARIONI HAD EXPECTED SOMETHING BETTER WHEN HE CAME FACE-to-face with Christine Lamont. A week earlier, her parents had made a brief trip to Brazil to comfort their daughter and try to sort out the mess she was in. Barioni had met them in his chambers. In an attempt to get an idea of the daughter's character, he had looked to her family, and he had liked what he had seen. Keith and Marilyn Lamont were clearly honest and hard-working people, and loving and dedicated parents. There was every reason to believe that the daughter they spoke of so fondly would come clean, tell everything she knew, and help police get to the bottom of the kidnapping. Barioni had warned the Lamonts that the case against Christine and David was very strong and could result in a conviction. He had hoped they would implore their daughter to cooperate. Obviously, his words, and perhaps theirs, had been in vain.

Barioni had formed the impression that Dr. and Mrs. Lamont thought that, by meeting with him, and by recruiting the help of the Canadian officials in São Paulo, they would somehow be able to fix things. They seemed to think that whatever had gone wrong could be corrected and that they could take their daughter home with them. They had made it clear, in particular, that they wanted their Christine released from the unpleasantness of prison, a place, they had assured him, in which their daughter did not belong. But Judge Barioni could not simply fix Christine's problems. He could not undo what she had done or return her to the condition in which her parents remembered her, as a naïve and idealistic student. The Lamonts left Brazil abruptly before the trial began, choosing to fight for Christine's freedom from Canada. Judge Barioni wished them well.

David Spencer took Christine Lamont's place before the judge on the first day in court. His testimony served only to compound the lies told by his girlfriend.

Christine Lamont had omitted any mention of the house rented by the pair on Rúa Pugliesi in her brief version of events. During David's account of what happened, he also neglected to mention the two and a half months they had spent living there. He went one step farther and told the judge that, before renting the house on Praca Hachiro Miyazaki, he and Christine had been living in a hotel on Avenida Julio in São Paulo.

Although at first glance the pair's stories seemed to coincide, the judge was able to weed out inconsistencies. The pair denied any knowledge that Abílio Diniz was being held captive in the basement of the house. Both said the first time they saw the man was when police surrounded the house and the victim was brought upstairs. Both claimed they barely knew their co-accused, even though they had been living with three of them for at least a month. But as the questions grew more specific, their testimonies began to differ. Christine said that she and David had nothing to do with their roommates, but David testified that he often cooked dinner for everyone in the house. He said that sometimes there were as many as twenty people over for a meal, and he cooked for all of them. Police believe David was referring to the team responsible for building the underground cell — again, part of the second team of kidnappers. Both testified that they had not been separated since their arrival in Latin America, but stamps on their false passports indicated that David Spencer had travelled to Uruguay on November 21 and stayed until November 24. Christine Lamont's fake passport showed that she had travelled to Argentina on November 29 and returned on December 2. Why the pair travelled separately to renew their Brazilian visas in their false names remains a mystery.

Testimony later in the trial led Barioni to conclude that the kidnapping plot was hatched and orchestrated from Argentina the previous summer, and the judge found it hard to believe that Christine's solo trip to that nation just days before Abílio Diniz was abducted was mere coincidence. David testified that he had met Humberto Paz in Argentina the previous summer, and the two had discussed the formation of a new political organization to help the poor and homeless in Latin America. David said he had been given Paz's name by a contact whom he declined to name. Paz, according to David, asked him if he would rent a house in São Paulo for other members of the organization to share with the Canadian couple. David said he agreed, but added that he had not even told his girlfriend about the political organization. Given that Christine, as Lisa Walker, had signed the lease on the first house, Judge Barioni chose not to accept David Spencer's attempts to exculpate her. He did not believe Christine was as much in the dark as her boyfriend claimed.

The judge repeatedly asked David Spencer if he had ever seen the white van that was disguised as an ambulance and used in the abduction. David said he had never seen the vehicle.

"Do you know why you were recognized as one of two people who took that car into the shop to be fixed on the eighth of December?" the judge asked.

"The only explanation I can give is that the person who was there must have made a mistake," David replied evenly.

"You were recognized by two people. Did two people make a mistake?"

"They must have because I am absolutely sure I never drove that vehicle," said David.

Both garage mechanics had pointed to David Spencer's picture when asked if they recognized any of the accused. Both said Spencer had accompanied Pedro Lembach to the garage for the second round of transmission repairs on the van.

As the questions became more specific, David Spencer's memory, like that of his girlfriend, began to fail.

From the indictment, David and his lawyers already knew that neighbours at the house on Praca Hachiro Miyazaki had told police they had seen him unloading wood and taking it into the house. He attempted to explain this to the judge.

"Did you do any work other than rent the house?"

"Once or twice I bought some construction materials," David answered.

"What kind of materials?"

"Wood and cement."

"Who delivered the materials?"

"I took them home myself."

"If that's the case, who did you give them to?"

"I took them and put them in the backyard."

"Didn't give them to anybody? Who asked you to buy them?"

"I don't remember."

"For what purpose did you buy these materials?"

"They never told me and I never asked. I think they were used for cabinets."

"Do you know carpentry?"

"No."

"Who did the work?"

"I can't remember, but I remember someone working in the back."

"How many days were they there?"

"I don't remember. Maybe a weekend."

"How many were there?"

"I can't say, I was always coming and going."

"Didn't you find it strange for these people to be working there?"

"No."

"Why did they call you 'Il Modesto'?' "

"It was a nickname I used."

David's reported nonchalance with respect to the construction at the rear of the house did not mesh with his earlier testimony that he hadn't really concerned himself with what this new, as yet unnamed political organization was doing. He said he had only been concerned that they not damage the house since he was the one who had signed the lease. Given this worry of his, David Spencer was now asking Judge Barioni to believe that he had not once wandered to the rear of the house to ask what his roommates were doing with the wood, cement, and other materials he had supplied free of charge.

When the judge asked David Spencer what he was doing with a false passport, he replied: "As protection against any future problems. I also did not want to use my real name because I have several debts in Canada." He offered no specifics about where he got his fake passport.

David Spencer ended his testimony with an account of the impressions Brazil's slums had upon a middle-class Canadian, and a plea to see the woman he loved.

"For someone growing up in Canadian society it's quite a shock to see your first shantytown in São Paulo. I don't think anyone could disagree that a situation where people find themselves living in these conditions certainly needs some kind of change," he told the judge. Then he asked that Christine be freed:

"She didn't know either about the existence of Mr. Diniz, much less the existence of the organization. We've been together some time, we have a good relationship, very close. But the less talked about it to Christine, the better, she didn't know what was going on and after we were arrested I couldn't talk to her. . . . I would like to ask if it's possible to see her, even if it's through glass?"

Barioni did not respond to David's request. The two were, in fact, able to spend a few short moments together outside the courtroom after they gave their testimony. The boy/man in front of Barioni sounded older than he looked, spoke with a cynicism and a sophistication that belied his youthful frame and mild voice. He was not instantly likeable, and his requests came across more as demands. Obviously, David Spencer felt he was entitled to see his girlfriend. Perhaps he had also felt he was entitled to take part in a kidnapping because he had satisfied himself that what he was doing was for a just cause.

CHAPTER 16

ASKING FOR IT

IN DECIDING TO STICK TO THEIR ORIGINAL STORIES THROUGHOUT their testimony, Christine and David contradicted themselves, each other, and the others accused. The trial judge guessed that the story was decided upon long before police surrounded the house and the siege began. The gang of kidnappers had pre-selected the people who would take the fall if they were caught, in the rather optimistic hope that the others would go free.

Humberto Paz, the Argentinian leader of the group, stood tall before Judge Barioni, his six-foot, four-inch, frame towering over both his interpreter and his lawyer. With a wide smile on his face and a gracious manner, he accepted complete responsibility for the kidnapping of Abílio Diniz. With obvious sincerity and no regrets, he confessed to planning and carrying out the actual kidnapping, and he named his brother Horácio and Raimundo Freire, the Brazilian guard, as his co-conspirators.

It was with apparent pride and triumph that he announced to Judge Barioni: "I took Abílio Diniz." The judge later described his tone — "as if, in a war, he had captured an enemy citadel."

Paz said others, such as David Spencer and Christine Lamont, knew only bits and pieces about the crime. David, for example, was used for logistical support, to rent the house and obtain supplies, such as the wood. Christine, Paz testified, didn't even know that much. By cooking and buying food, she had inadvertently become the supplier for the kidnappers.

Paz was engaging in a very crude form of damage control, trying to get as many of the accused off as possible. The prosecution was not alleging that Christine and David were among the kidnappers. But, given that witnesses had placed at least five people at the actual kidnapping scene — not just the three whom Paz was willing to implicate — Barioni knew for certain that he was lying.

In his summation, Barioni later wrote of Paz's testimony: "Everything [had been] previously and carefully thought out and agreed on perhaps even before the nearly forty hours of surrender negotiations that Humberto spent inside the house on Praca Hachiro Miyazaki, together with five other defendants."

Humberto Paz is an inherently likeable man, with an easy manner and jovial air. He is also ruthless. Brazilian police, with the help of their Argentinian counterparts, implicated Paz in the slaughter of seven soldiers and one police officer in the failed assault on La Tablada army garrison just ten months earlier.

Paz's methods were repulsive, but even Judge Barioni found his motivation to be genuine. Paz assured the judge that the accused were acting for political change, not personal gain.

"Neither I nor any of the persons accused would ever commit a crime for their personal advantage," Paz told Barioni near the end of his testimony.

When the defendants stood before Judge Barioni in the following days, each in turn gave his version of events. Aside from Humberto and Horácio Paz, and the guard, Raimundo Freire, they all claimed that they were knowingly involved with a new political organization aimed at changing the status quo in Latin America, and each also claimed he knew nothing about the kidnapping. Like Christine and David had done, each began to tell a slightly different story under close examination. Since none knew what the co-accused had testified, they were unable to corroborate one another's stories in detail, which strengthened Barioni's suspicion that their testimony had been worked out ahead of time.

The Chilean, Hector Ramón Collante Tapia, one of the suspects in the house during the siege, testified that it had taken him at least a month to build Abílio Diniz's cell and the small adjacent room for Raimundo Freire. Tapia painted himself to be a humble labourer hired by Humberto Paz to build a wine cellar in a basement. This contradicted David Spencer's assertion that construction lasted only a weekend. Barioni was later to conclude that a construction project dragged out over a month could hardly have gone unnoticed by the occupants of the house in which it was taking place, and rejected Christine and David's claim to the contrary.

Barioni painstakingly pieced together the organization that went into the preparations for the kidnapping. In many ways, he concluded, Christine and David formed the advance party. Being North American meant that they would have less trouble securing a fairly large home at a substantial rent. But their task was not minor: its successful completion would prove vital. Their instructions most likely included finding not only accommodations, but also transportation, and also planning the escape, which is perhaps one of the reasons David bought a Kombi van that he rarely used. Neighbours remembered seeing him wash mud and dirt out of the back of the little white truck after dark. Police later guessed that he was hauling away the dirt and debris from the underground construction project.

Hector Tapia's passport showed that he had arrived in Brazil from Chile just four days after Christine and David had rented their first house, on Rúa Pugliesi. He also had a part to play in the early preparations. He was to help Christine and David get the kidnap house ready. Police suspect he was one of the workmen at the Rúa Pugliesi house. When the abduction was delayed because a policeman lived across the street, Hector Tapia sat idle until the couple rented the second house. This time they would not bar the front of the house with wood and risk arousing suspicion among their neighbours. They did put up an awning, build a small fence, and move some large plants in front of the garage to block the view. But their new strategy was to keep their victim hidden underground.

Romeu Tuma, Jr., would later wonder out loud in talking to reporters about whether or not the kidnappers, in coming up with their plan to hold Abílio in the underground crypt, had literally taken a page from a then-recent thriller by the British novelist Frederick Forsyth. Forsyth's book *The Negotiator* was first released in the spring of 1989, eight months before Abílio was kidnapped. The story, which revolves around the bargaining skills of a hostage negotiator, describes a kidnapping committed in broad daylight in which the victim is thrown into the back of a disguised van and taken to an unassuming house in a middle-class neighbourhood. The description of the underground cell in which he is imprisoned, complete with ventilation, a portable toilet, and a peephole in the door, is virtually identical with that of Abílio Diniz's holding cell at 149 Praca Hachiro Miyazaki. The reason Forsyth suggests for building a subterranean hiding-place is that the search for obvious isolation by those assigned to find a safehouse, be it a country house or a walled compound, would be remembered by real estate agents, who, in turn, might pass the information on if questioned by police. An average house on an average street with no outward signs of unusual security is more likely to pass from the memory of anyone who had contact with the kidnappers.

Another detail found both in Forsyth's book and in the real-life kidnapping is the kidnappers' communicating with the victim only through notes, with the result that the victim is unable to identify his captors by either voice or accent. Disciplined silence was the modus operandi of both the fictional and the real gang.

When they were searching for a house where an underground room could easily be installed, Christine and David made a trip to the city water and sewer department. A deep, silent pit already in place would save them both time and effort and, with the delay caused by having to relocate, they were already behind schedule. But the new plan also called for unanticipated extra work. Dry wells are not ventilated, and fresh air had to be piped in, using an electric generator. This was placed directly above Abílio Diniz's "tank," as the judge called it. The modifications became the responsibility of Hector Tapia. Tapia claimed that he did not know that the room was intended for a man; he thought it was meant to be a wine cellar. David Spencer, meanwhile, claimed complete ignorance of the tiny compartment. He told Barioni that he and Christine had never noticed the generator or heard the loud noise it made. Nor, apparently, did they ever notice the speaker installed in the kitchen, which was connected to a microphone in Diniz's cell so that the people in the house could hear any unusual activity on the part of their victim.

Through testimony, Barioni was able to piece together the plan that had taken shape. The second and third teams of experienced terrorists had moved in on Brazil's largest city. They slipped into the country with false passports and rented modest hotel suites across the city. They were getting ready: they knew their target, and the first team had seen to it that all necessary preparations had been made. It was just a matter of time.

Throughout the trial, the strength of the case against the gang of kidnappers grew daily, as did the list of witnesses, each with his or her own version of events to pass along to Judge Barioni, some in person, others in sworn statements. Neighbours described watching the young foreign couple orchestrate the camouflage of the front of both the first house they rented and the kidnap house on

Praca Hachiro Miyazaki. Another neighbour told Barioni that, shortly after moving in to the second house, Christine had queried her son about what his parents did for a living. Others stated that a young blonde woman had bought the van used in the abduction. Different neighbours described Christine as being blonde when she moved into the couple's second house. The garage mechanics pointed to David as the man who had brought the white minivan in for repairs just days before the kidnapping. The private chauffeur who had witnessed the abduction helped finger the kidnappers who took part. Another eye-witness to the kidnapping, who was standing some distance away, told the judge what he remembered. The scores of police officers involved in the investigation, and then the siege, explained what had happened. Abílio Diniz himself told the judge of his horror inside the cage underground. "I was certain I would die," Abílio said.

As the trial wound down and the publicity mounted, Judge Barioni was left to the lonely task of looking towards a verdict and trying to decide how to mete out fair punishment.

CHAPTER 17

BRAZIL'S GROWTH INDUSTRY

IT WOULD BE THE BEGINNING OF MAY 1990 BEFORE A JUDGEMENT would be handed down. No one who had followed the trial was expecting acquittals. Even the lawyers representing the ten accused had conceded that the evidence against their clients was overwhelming.

The defence's strategy was two-pronged. First, they had worked to get some of the accused, including Christine and David, acquitted unconditionally on the basis that they hadn't known enough of the total plan to be found guilty of the crime they were charged with, even though they had committed some illegal acts. But a large part of the defence's arguments were aimed at getting Barioni to move the case to Federal Court, claiming that the crime was political. The strategy here was to admit some guilt on the part of all ten accused, who were represented by the same two respected human-rights lawyers recommended by Dom Paulo Evaristo Cardinal Arns, since a charge of having committed a political crime would bring much shorter sentences.

During the course of the trial, Judge Barioni heard that, when the kidnappers had chosen Abílio Diniz as their victim, they had drawn on detailed research conducted by their advance team over a considerable period of time. Abílio Diniz was described in their briefing notes as "abusive and arrogant" — arrogant enough, in any case, to snub his nose at security, to defiantly drive his two Mercedeses past the poverty-stricken street children of São Paulo as he tooled around the city, to walk alone on dangerous city streets, and to refuse to turn his home into a prison and his family into captives of their own success. He was also physically very fit and, in the judgment of his abductors, could withstand the rigours of captivity better than some of the other potential victims. Just one month prior to his kidnapping, Abílio had competed in a triathalon amid a field of much younger men.

At one bizarre point in their final arguments, lawyers Belisario dos Santos and Marco Antonio Nahum introduced the idea that his lack of security made Abílio Diniz a nearly voluntary victim.

> Here, for lack of food, infant mortality rates are among the highest in the world. Slums proliferate. Illiteracy is growing. There is misery on an alarming scale. . . . In sharp contrast to this macabre scene is the image of the victim, Mr. Abílio dos Santos Diniz, a man whose almost daily promotion in the media presents him as one of the most powerful people in the nation. The daily newspapers say he owns two Mercedes-Benz cars — one a dark blue sports model and the other white — and a yacht that would have been the envy of the late Onassis, that he has assets of about U.S.$180 million, and that he is about to build a bank with the brand name Diniz. . . . despite this public posture, which is at the very least unusual, he never uses personal security. . . . such behaviour characterizes Mr. Abílio dos Santos Diniz beyond all doubt as a propitiatory victim.

In essence, the lawyers tried to convince Judge Barioni that Abílio Diniz had been "asking for it." They called their theory "victimology" and, in presenting it to the court, implied that Diniz deserved the fate he had endured at the hands of his captors. Diniz had, in fact, spent the harrowing hours of his captivity wondering what exactly he had done to deserve such treatment. It seems that wealth had been his crime. And judgement was passed in an underground cage.

The lawyers' tactics were to give Barioni options from which to choose in reaching his verdict. By presenting a rigorous, multifaceted defence, they also left doors open for various appeals to be launched.

In the hope of gaining reduced sentences, the lawyers then presented their theory that the crime fell within Brazil's political crimes division, crimes punishable by much lighter sentences than those carried out for personal gain. But, despite their best efforts, the defence lawyers could not prove that the kidnapping of Abílio Diniz was somehow linked to plans to destabilize the Brazilian government. Without posing a direct threat to the government of the day, the kidnapping could not be classified as a political crime. The lawyers had also argued that, if the kidnapping was political, then it did not fall within the São Paulo jurisdiction of Judge Barioni, and should be transferred to the Federal Court in Brasilia. Barioni ruled against both of these proposals, citing cases in Brazilian law that showed this kidnapping to be neither a federal crime nor a political crime against the nation, although he added that he felt the accused had been politically motivated.

"If they were being sincere [in their political motivations], they were using their resources in Chile and Argentina and not in Brazil," Barioni stated.

He went on to say that, unless the crime itself or the proceeds from the crime, were aimed at overthrowing the Brazilian government — and there was no proof that this was the case — then they could not be tried under Brazil's National Security Law, but rather as ordinary criminals.

Barioni's judgement reflected his thoughts on the crime itself, and showed some sympathy with the kidnappers, some of whom had convinced him that their final goal was to help others. He alluded to a Robin Hood mentality among the accused. He also spoke frankly of the pressure he was under to bring in convictions against all ten accused on all charges, including resisting arrest for those who had remained in the kidnap house during the siege, and the crime of gangsterism, on which they all faced charges for having formed an organized, armed movement.

Perhaps moved by the explanations of Humberto Paz, and particularly of Maria Badilla (Rubia), who described the shame of infant mortality and widespread illiteracy to Judge Barioni, the judge found some leeway. He concluded that the gang was not organized enough to be considered guilty of formal gangsterism, especially since police had not uncovered any one name for the group, although the ties to other formal groups had been well established. He also dismissed the charges of resisting arrest faced by the six accused who had been in the kidnap house during the siege, saying that refusing to leave a house did not constitute resistance. But when it came to the charges of conspiracy to kidnap, none of the accused could be let off. Every one of them had been caught out in several lies. Not one of them had been willing to identify for the judge the others involved in the crime or how they could be tracked down. Not one of them had broken the disciplined silence for which they were now well known.

The judge blasted the defence's "victimology" strategy that somehow found Abílio Diniz deserving of such treatment because he did not employ a personal army to protect him and his family.

"Abílio Diniz is not 'guilty' of being a millionaire. . . . Abílio Diniz had and still has, like all of us, the right to go about without security and not be molested," said the judge. He went on to suggest that the defence itself was almost grounds enough for him to increase the penalty handed down to the accused.

"I can argue that the fact that Abílio Diniz is so widely known, so prominent a figure in the country, made the crime an act that attracted very great publicity, to the point of provoking popular outcry at the national level, and hence that the defendants deserve a more severe reprimand."

Considering the possible sentences of twenty-five years that the gang faced, they all expressed relief when Barioni handed down sentences of from eight to fifteen years for all of them. Christine Lamont, for her role in providing logistical support, but recognizing that she did not actually take part in the abduction, was sentenced to eight years in prison. In his written judgement, Barioni picks apart the lies in her testimony: "Nor is it believable — this applies also to David — that she [Christine] did not know about the veritable arsenal of weapons and ammunition seized in the house where she was living."

The judge decided that David Spencer was more deeply involved in the planning of the crime, and from an earlier stage. He accordingly was given a ten-year sentence.

"David's version is completely unacceptable. His statements are contradictory and vague. He impressed me as more cynical than Humberto [Paz]. . . . I take into account David's important role in the preparations for the kidnapping . . . he worked for a long period in connection with the kidnapping, at least from the beginning of August 1989, when he rented the house on Rúa Francisco Pugliesi. This points to strong evil intent and therefore his penalty cannot be set at the legal minimum."

Humberto Paz was sentenced to fifteen years in jail for being what Barioni described as "a true public menace because he is able to rally and coordinate a considerable number of people . . . he spent an enormous amount of time on preparation for the crime, indicative of long premeditation and hence of strong evil intent."

Despite the light sentences, the defence immediately announced that it would appeal the convictions, pursuing its theory that the crime should have been termed political and tried in Federal Court, while the prosecution revealed plans to appeal the sentences, considered light compared to the twenty-five years that they had asked for.

Lawyer Marco Antonio Nahum told reporters after the sentences were handed down that both Christine and David, who, like all of the accused in the Brazilian justice system, were not in court when the judgement was read, were pleased with their relatively light jail terms. All of the accused were also fined varying amounts, depending on their involvment in the crime. David was fined $8,400, and Christine $1,800.

In his written judgement, Barioni spoke of the numerous references he had received attesting to Christine's good character.

> The case documents contain a number of statements by qualified persons attesting that Christine is a very good and lovable person. A professor of Latin American history at Simon Fraser University attested that Christine studied there for three or four years and devoted a great deal of time and energy to presenting information on contemporary issues in Latin America, as a holder of high moral principles. An accountant testified that she is of excellent family, her father being a doctor. The family's businesses included a medical clinic, an incorporated medical company, a medical administration company, and a music instruction school. Her mother is a music teacher. Finally, I obtained an excellent impression of her parents. All these circumstances will be taken into account in sentencing, since her guilt is inescapable.

For Judge Barioni, glowing references and kind parents were not enough to refute the guilt of Christine Lamont.

Barioni's original sentence called for what is known as "open custody," allowing Christine and David to be released from solitary confinement and integrated with the general prison population. At first, it also looked as though Brazil's parole laws would enable the pair to spend only between two and three years behind bars before being eligible for either daytime release, allowing them to work outside the prison, or full parole. But this didn't happen. A review of their situation by their lawyers revealed that, as foreigners, they would not be eligible for parole at all. In fact, both were kept in solitary confinement for lengthy periods of time, at the discretion of the prison wardens, who claimed to fear for the safety of the kidnappers in the general population after all the notoriety they had achieved during the trial.

As their months in jail passed, the appeals process moved slowly. Christine and David's lawyers were moving on two fronts to get the ten accused a better deal. They were appealing the sentences to the higher court in São Paulo, and at the same time launching an appeal to Brazil's Federal Court challenging the constitutionality of the convictions on the basis that, as the lawyers still maintained, the case should not have been heard at the lower-court level in the first place. In hindsight, Christine and David's families said that using the same two lawyers for all the accused had not been a wise choice. Christine and David's interests were not the sole responsibility of their lawyers, who also had the others to think of in making their arguments. But, after their arrest, the Canadian couple had decided to go with the legal counsel recommended by Archbishop Arns, a man whom they felt they could trust.

True to his word, Abílio Diniz set up a fund to pay for the initial legal defence fees of the ten accused, although not any appeals. When news first broke that Diniz would pay for the defence, several high-profile lawyers refused to take the case, saying they were worried about the ethical problems posed by money coming from the victim himself. But Belisario dos Santos and Marco Antonio

Nahum agreed to take the case at the urging of the archbishop, and no one ever questioned the integrity of the kidnappers' two lawyers, who are both well respected in their field.

The impact of the kidnapping in Brazil did not die down with time. A man named Luiz Antonio Fleury Fihlo saw to it that no one in the state of São Paulo forgot that police had snared a band of international terrorists and saved the life of a respected businessman. Fleury, who was state secretary of São Paulo's Public Security at the time of the kidnapping and arrest, the de facto head government official in the case, was running for governor of the state of São Paulo in late 1990, almost a year after Abílio Diniz's abduction.

The successful negotiations for the release of Abílio Diniz were a feather in Fleury's cap. He wasted no opportunity to remind Brazilians that it was under his leadership that justice had been done. During his election campaign, Fleury presented himself as the only viable law-and-order candidate to the millions of São Paulo residents who lived in constant fear of thugs in the streets. The now-famous picture of the ten convicts in the Diniz case, lined up side by side in shackles in the São Paulo police station, was used on campaign posters that lined the subways, bus stops, and highway billboards in São Paulo. No one was given a chance to forget who these people were and the danger they represented, a danger that Fleury himself claimed to have reined in. Politicians being what they are the world over, Fleury took credit for the work of others. His role in securing Abílio Diniz's release was minor, although he was present during the siege and he was the man formally in charge. The kidnapping did end peacefully, and with the arrest and conviction of those responsible. Almost a year later, when the ballots were counted in the race for governor, Luiz Antonio Fleury's astute politicking carried him smoothly into São Paulo's governor's mansion.

By the time the São Paulo higher court agreed to hear the

appeals of the convicted kidnappers, close to two years had passed since the abduction. The early hopes that Christine and David had entertained of being able to serve their time in minimum-security prisons or half-way houses, or on day parole, were dashed with the news that foreigners are ineligible for parole of any sort in Brazil. By this time the Canadians, along with their fellow convicts, had been a part of the general prison population for months and had taken on various jobs within the prison; Christine was working in the sewing room, and David worked as a janitor. Both told a Vancouver newspaper reporter that they spent this time in hopeful anticipation that their situation would change, that they would have their sentences thrown out, or at the very least they would be granted some form of parole.

When the news finally came to them via their lawyers on December 2, 1991, it was not what they had expected. The prosecution had won its appeal of the shorter sentences. The three-judge tribunal of the Supreme Court of São Paulo had upheld the kidnapping convictions and brought in convictions on the charges of gangsterism and resisting arrest. The maximum penalty for each crime was imposed on all the accused. The end result for Christine and David was a stunning twenty-eight years behind bars in their respective São Paulo prisons.

Once again, the severity of the sentences would not be eased by Brazil's parole laws. But, in handing down their decision, the judges did mention a provision in the constitution that called for foreigners to be expelled from the country after their sentences are up. This was interpreted by many as meaning that Brazil's parole laws, which usually allow a prisoner to be released after one third of his or her sentence had been served, would be used as a guideline for when foreigners would be expelled from Brazil and returned to their homeland.

The reasons for the harshness of the sentences were clear to anyone who had being paying attention to events in Brazil. In the months since the Diniz abduction, kidnapping for ransom in Brazil had reached epidemic proportions. The outbreak was prompted in large part by the anti-inflationary measures of the victorious presidential candidate, Fernando Collor de Mello, who had swept into power on the same day that the siege at the kidnap house had come to an end. The new government froze up to 80 per cent of the country's bank accounts, creating a cash-flow problem for the law-abiding, and chaos for the nation's considerable criminal element. Criminals desperate for cash that they could not simply steal turned to kidnapping as a source of income. The government allowed families access to their bank accounts if they needed money to pay a ransom demand. The result was thousands of kidnappings, not only of the very wealthy, but of the middle class.

In São Paulo, the number of kidnappings soared to almost four hundred in the year following the Diniz abduction. Children of local merchants were being kidnapped on their way home from school, and businessmen from every walk of life stopped arriving home after work. Sometimes the criminals did not even need to plan and execute the kidnapping; they simply picked a target and sent a note saying that the target's children would be next if payment wasn't made. A demand for ransom was a justifiable reason to free up money locked safely in the country's banks, and career criminals were using these threats to create a regular source of income. In one week in 1991 in the tourist capital of Rio de Janeiro, more than thirty people were abducted. Outraged residents of Brazil's large cities were demanding that the army be called in to restore order, and there was talk among legislators of introducing the death penalty for convicted kidnappers.

It was against this background that the judicial tribunal in São Paulo came to its decision. It chose to set a fierce example for anyone contemplating an abduction like that of Abílio Diniz. Judge Jarbas Mazzoni wrote:

> Presently, because of its frequency, the crime of kidnapping for ransom . . . constitutes a constant alarm in our country.
>
> In effect, it is necessary to put an end to the feeling of impunity which encourages these criminals. Moved by greed, they do not hesitate to hold their victims captive, in an inhumane manner, subjecting them to physical and mental torture, which also extend to their family members. It is necessary to put an end to the actions of these criminals who, moved by greed, do not hesitate to terrorize Brazilian homes, turning our country into a haven for kidnappers. . . .

Many Brazilians felt angry and besieged. Their children were being threatened and they were helpless to do anything but hand over the sums demanded. They wanted a tough stance by the courts, and the judges were more than willing to give them one. The crime of kidnapping disgusted everyone — everyone, that is, except for the proponents of Brazil's newest growth industry, the kidnappers themselves.

PART III:
The Crusade

CHAPTER 18

A BOLT OUT OF THE BLUE

THE PHONE CALL TO THE LAMONT HOME ON DECEMBER 2, 1991, bringing news of the extended jail terms, marked the second time in less than two years that news from Brazil had sent the Lamont family reeling.

It had been a trying, difficult two years in which the family had experienced a roller-coaster ride of emotional high and lows, from momentary relief and hope to deep sadness and bitter anger. There had been few reasons to feel grateful and plenty of reasons for sharp criticism, both of what was happening in Brazil and what was not happening at home, in Canada.

News of the original arrest had come just days before Christmas 1989 as Marilyn was sitting in the family's dining-room, addressing Christmas cards to their many friends and business associates. The phone had rung just after 3:00 p.m. on a wet, west-coast Sunday afternoon. The message had been abrupt: someone you love is in trouble — deep trouble.

Keith had been upstairs in the family's sprawling, ranch-style house when he heard the phone ring and his wife answer the phone. Within seconds, Marilyn was yelling for Keith to pick up the upstairs extension. Keith had no time to register the panic in her voice.

The woman on the other end of the line was calling from the External Affairs building on Sussex Drive in Ottawa, just steps from the opulent official residence of Canada's prime minister. The caller told Keith and Marilyn that she had been asked to contact them by the Canadian consulate in São Paulo, Brazil. She had received news that a woman giving the name Christine Gwen Lamont and an address in Langley, British Columbia, had been arrested in connection with a kidnapping. Her identity had not been verified by local police, but she had given the Lamonts' phone number to a consular official and asked that they be notified. The official had few details to offer, but gave the Lamonts the name and number of Pierre Pichette, the Canadian consular official who had witnessed the woman's surrender and arrest. The night-duty officer at External Affairs told the Lamonts that they would be contacted as more details on their daughter's plight became available.

Keith's first reaction was that one of their friends, perhaps one of the people to whom Marilyn was in the process of addressing a cheery Christmas card, was playing a joke. Keith didn't find it amusing.

"Actually, at one point, I wanted to hang up on her because I was getting tired of this little joke," he later told a reporter from a Vancouver newspaper.

But as they gradually came to understand that the phone call was not a prank, the Lamonts begged for more information and assurances that Christine was all right. The External Affairs official had only scant details to offer them, she was able to tell them that Christine had been arrested with several other people, including one other Canadian, who gave the name David Robert Spencer and an address in Moncton, New Brunswick.

The Lamonts called Christine's sisters, Elisabeth and Heather, and her brother, Mark, to break the news. That Christine was in trouble did not come as a complete shock to the Lamonts. Some weeks earlier, in mid-November, fearing for his daughter's safety, Keith had called an old chum from the University of Manitoba's basketball team. He had asked Dr. Carl Ridd, a Professor of Religious Studies in Winnipeg, if he had any suggestions on how Keith and Marilyn could track down Christine, who Keith had then described as "missing." Dr. Ridd had been through a similar nightmare just weeks earlier when his own daughter, twenty-eight-year-old Karen Ridd, had been detained for twelve hours while doing aid work in El Salvador with the human-rights group Peace Brigade. Karen Ridd had earned herself the title of hero after she had been told she could go by the feared Treasury Police but refused to leave her prison without a fellow worker, a Colombian national, who had been arrested with Ridd. Karen Ridd had stood up for what she believed in the face of what could have been deadly danger. Her stance had won the freedom of her colleague, perhaps saving the woman's life. She had been ordered released after Canadian diplomats from nearby Costa Rica arrived to demand an explanation. Ridd's capture and subsequent release became a national story in Canada and had planted fears in Keith and Marilyn's minds that something similar might happen to Christine. As it turned out, the Lamonts' worries about Christine had been alleviated when she had telephoned on November 29 to wish her sister Heather a happy birthday. She had told them that she and David were heading to Argentina for a couple of weeks, but had supplied no specifics. The Lamonts were left with the impression that Christine and David were taking a low-budget Christmas holiday from their long days working as translators in Managua.

On the other side of the country, it was 7:00 p.m. and darkness had already fallen on a cold, snowy evening, when Bill Spencer took his phone call in his comfortable bungalow, aglow with Christmas lights, in Moncton.

"I was numb, I really was. I don't know if it sank in right away. I guess it has to sink in eventually. You just feel so helpless," he said afterwards.

For the seventy-one-year-old grandfather of two, the call was a harsh blow in a year in which he'd already buried his wife, leaving him alone for the first time after more than forty years of marriage.

As phone lines from Brazil and Ottawa carried the news of Christine and David's fate to the Lamont dining-room and Bill Spencer's kitchen, news wires and satellites were sending images of the mysterious Canadians, hands raised in surrender, as they walked out of the kidnap house. Every media outlet in Canada jumped to attention and took up the chase for more information on what Brazilians were calling "Canada's terrorists."

By early the next morning, the phone in Langley began to ring. The media had come calling — en masse. Reporters across the country scrambled for a different angle on the story. Those based on the West Coast went directly to the Lamont family for details about Christine. The family, caught off guard by the barrage of callers, did their best to provide reporters with the few answers they had as to how their middle daughter had ended up shackled to her boyfriend and paraded in front of Brazilian journalists.

"We just don't understand what's going on. This just doesn't seem in character with our daughter," Marilyn said.

She didn't have much to offer by way of answers. They hadn't even been able to reach trade commissioner Pierre Pichette by the time they took the first call from a Canadian Press reporter.

"I don't know how long she's been in Brazil," Marilyn said. "I can't really talk about it until after we talk to the consul."

But when the Lamonts finally got through to Pichette, he could not shed much new light on their daughter's predicament.

"I told them that I had been there for the surrender and I had gone with Christine and David to the police station. But I told them that neither of them had said anything to me about what they were doing in Brazil, or in that house. They all stayed very quiet, the whole group of them," he said later.

Pichette did not tell the Lamonts about their daughter's steely, determined stare, or about David Spencer's defiant silence after the pair had curtly supplied him with their names and the phone numbers of their parents. The Canadians, following the lead of their co-accused, stared straight ahead as they were marched before television cameras at a news conference in an elegant conference room at the São Paulo police headquarters. Their wrists were handcuffed together, Christine's and David's fingers intertwined.

Pierre Pichette stayed with the Canadians at the police station for several hours. He stayed to see the arrival of the well-known São Paulo lawyers who, at the beckoning of the archbishop, Dom Paulo Evaristo Cardinal Arns, were to provide representation for the accused as part of the deal worked out with Abílio Diniz. Pichette then asked the head investigator with the anti-kidnapping squad if his assistance was still required and was assured that the situation was under control, but that he was welcome to return first thing the next morning should the Canadians require anything further from the consul.

"I felt they would be fine, there was no threat of danger to them at all. The police had solved the kidnapping, everyone was very calm and almost relaxed. If I thought there would be any problem, I never would have gone home. But that wasn't the case."

On Monday morning, accompanied by Consul General William Ross, Pichette returned to the police station and once again met separately with the Canadians for a brief visit. The two men asked the pair if they were all right and if they could pass along any messages to their families. Both Christine and David said they had been well treated and were pleased with the lawyers recommended by the archbishop, one of whom spoke English, which was a great relief for the Canadians. They were tired, after being kept up all night for questioning and processing. William Ross said later that, despite the questioning, the pair seemed well: "They appeared to be in good spirits. They said they were fine, and had not been mistreated in any way."

David asked Pichette to pass a message to his father, requesting that the elder Spencer not discuss David or the case with the media. Later that same morning, Pichette spoke with both Bill Spencer and the Lamonts, telling them that their children were well but had again declined to discuss any details of the kidnapping. He told Bill Spencer about his son's request. The elder Spencer sent a telegram to his son in which he stated that he would keep quiet and not divulge information to the Canadian media. With this seemingly simple message, the grieving and shocked Bill Spencer inadvertently set off a feeding frenzy among the Brazilian media. A guard in the São Paulo prison complex, to which Christine and David had been transferred on Monday night, let out word that one of the accused in the Diniz kidnapping had received a warning by telegram from Canada to "shut up." These were neither the words nor the gist of Bill Spencer's message, but rather a clumsy attempt at translation; nonetheless, they prompted front-page headlines in Brazil and, in turn, wire-copy stories in Canada.

The fuss made life a bit harder for both Christine's and David's families as the media scrutiny of the pair intensified. Then, when news reached Canada two days after the arrest that Christine and David were carrying false passports bearing the names Lisa Lynne Walker and Paul Joseph Gomez Mendes, the questions became even harder for the Lamont family to answer.

The day after the arrest, Marilyn told a *Globe and Mail* reporter that she didn't know why her daughter was in Brazil, and added that the arrest of Christine and David Spencer "comes as a bolt out of the blue." She also told the reporter that Christine had been working as a translator in Managua, Nicaragua, for almost a year.

To *Toronto Star* reporter Dale Brazao, Marilyn said much the same thing. "I'm absolutely astounded. It's not at all like Chris," she said, adding that they thought Christine had been in Nicaragua, working as a translator, until she called to tell them she was heading to Argentina for a couple of weeks' vacation. "She was in Argentina when she phoned here two weeks ago. She didn't mention anything about Brazil."

Christine's sisters also expressed surprise. Elisabeth told a West Coast magazine, "We didn't even know she was in Brazil," and Heather said she knew of Christine's work in Central America, but Brazil was a complete surprise: "She was involved in human rights for Central America, especially El Salvador, but she had never been to South America."

The Lamonts also contacted their lawyer in B.C., seeking help. His advice was that of lawyers everywhere — offer no comment to the media until you're sure you know what's happening.

"We've decided to say we're shocked that this has happened, we don't understand it," said Elisabeth.

By Monday night, a little more than twenty-four hours after the arrest, the Lamont family had started to build Christine's defence — and make her excuses.

Worn down by the persistent images of Christine and David as terrorists that had now reached the television sets of Canadians from coast to coast, Heather was the first to speak out.

"I know them. They are both kind, caring people. They are not terrorists." Heather Lamont said that the media had presented a "very distorted picture of the couple. They are both concerned with human rights, [which is] not the picture that they [news media] are portraying."

At the same time, the family revealed how little they knew about Christine's activities. Marilyn Lamont was unable to tell *The Globe and Mail* whether or not her daughter had graduated from Simon Fraser University. No one in the family could identify any of the human-rights activities Christine and David had been involved with, or name any groups or people with whom they might have worked in preparation for their trip to Latin America. Reporters contacted various aid organizations with offices in Vancouver, including Amnesty International, in search of anyone who might give official sanction to Christine and David's human-rights activities. No one who was contacted had heard of the pair. No one from Salvaide or the El Salvador Information Office came forward to acknowledge the pair's previous work with the group.

"I'm not sure what David does," Heather Lamont said. "He's my sister's boyfriend. We don't understand what's happening. This is all very hard for us to understand. We don't know what she was doing."

In interview after interview, no member of the Lamont family reported having had any idea that Christine and David had been anywhere other than Nicaragua, except for their reported holiday to Argentina.

In Langley, upstanding citizens lined up to tell reporters that they would personally attest to the character of Christine's parents. Keith Lamont, head of surgery at Langley Memorial Hospital, had been a recipient of Langley's "Citizen of the Year" award. Marilyn, an accomplished pianist, had founded and taught at a local music school which had grown to become the third-largest in the province. Both were known for generously donating their time and resources to help the small farming community that had grown in recent years to become a bedroom community for commuters to Vancouver, less than an hour away. Former Langley mayor Reg Easingwood attested to the family's good character, but admitted that he did not know Christine well. "I can imagine the shock they must have had. The father is an excellent surgeon and the mother an accomplished pianist. They are really solid citizens."

George Preston, family friend and another former mayor, and owner of a local car dealership, said the local girl he remembered could not be the kidnapping suspect.

"I don't think she could ever hurt anybody. She wanted to go down there to Latin America to help people, not hurt them," he said. "The girl you tell me about isn't the girl I know. That's just not her style. Generally, she was a very quiet girl. I'm really very surprised about this."

Neighbours and friends described Keith and Marilyn as "devastated" by the news, and by the realization that their months of worry about their daughter's activities had been justified.

"I think in the back of their minds they had a fear that something like this would happen after they didn't hear from her for so long," said one long-time family friend.

On the east coast, Bill Spencer took refuge from the media and heeded his son's request for silence in the Moncton home of daughter Judy, seven years David's senior, and her husband, Mike, an insurance broker, and their two young daughters, Kristina and Nicola. Together, they grappled with the idea of twenty-six-year-old David as a terrorist and a kidnapper.

Bill Spencer had been contacted by Marilyn and Keith Lamont on the night they had received the news. They had said they were in the process of deciding which family members should go down to Brazil to ensure that Christine was all right and asked if one of the Spencers planned to make the trip. Bill Spencer was living on a pension and could not easily afford the airfare to Brazil. He was also more than a decade older than the Lamonts and just didn't feel he was up to travelling thousands of kilometres to face the agony and heartbreak of seeing his youngest child sitting helplessly behind bars. He told the Lamonts that he would not be making the trip.

Reporters in Moncton had by this time tracked down some old acquaintances of David Spencer. His former teachers said he was very much your average student, nothing noteworthy about him. Another person who had known David during his days in Moncton remembered the transformation to punker and said he had taken up with a "hippie crowd." Another described him as a "throwback to the flower-power generation." This wasn't the norm for a young man from Moncton, but it certainly wasn't the makings of an international terrorist.

As Bill Spencer sat and worried and waited for External Affairs to update him on the charges his son faced, Marilyn and Keith Lamont renewed their passports and booked a flight to Brazil. They would arrive in São Paulo first thing Thursday, December 21, and look for some answers. Plans for a family Christmas had long since been forgotten. The Lamonts were about to fly to another hemisphere, another country, and another world. It was a world in which their much-loved daughter was behind bars for a crime that repelled a nation — a crime the people of Brazil, both rich and poor, continued to focus on through the media as the days passed and the intrigue mounted.

CHAPTER 19

CONNECTIONS

IN VANCOUVER, BRITISH COLUMBIA, OFFICERS IN THE RCMP detachment were looking for answers of their own. They had been asked to investigate the mysterious passports of two B.C. residents and to check the backgrounds of Christine and David as a courtesy to the Brazilian authorities who were looking into the kidnapping.

Two constables arrived at the suburban front door of Lisa Lynne Walker, a housewife, mother of two boys — Lee and Dustin — and wife of Jack. In her small, comfortable Aldergrove home, the casually dressed and perpetually perky Mrs. Walker didn't fit the bill of a woman aiding and abetting kidnappers half a world away. She also didn't want to talk to the police. At first, she wasn't willing to discuss how a passport in her name had showed up in Christine Lamont's possession in São Paulo. Walker said she didn't know where her passport was, even though she'd obtained it just six months ago. Only after Lisa Walker was apprised of the criminality of selling or trading in Canadian passports did she reluctantly tell investigators that she and Christine Lamont were old friends.

When a Vancouver newspaper tracked her down, Lisa Walker said she had no idea how her passport came to be in Brazil.

"This has been very upsetting for everybody," Walker said. "She is a good friend. This is completely out of character [for Christine], and it's a complete shock."

When police told Walker they had confirmed that the passport found in the kidnapping house in Brazil was the same one that had been issued to her, she said she found that hard to believe. RCMP officers again assured her that this was the case and asked her if she had any explanation. Walker told police she had gone sometime the previous spring to the Vancouver passport office and applied for a passport for the first time. Police also questioned Walker as to why she chose not to have her two young sons, Lee and Dustin, put on her passport, as is customary with young children, but officers say they got no clear answer. Police felt that Walker, who is close to the entire Lamont family, was nervous that she might say something that would worsen Christine's situation, even though she obviously knew very little about Christine's recent activities.

Walker told police that Christine had popped in for an afternoon while she was home visiting her parents the previous spring. She said the pair had looked through old photo albums, and she speculated that she might have left her passport in the front of one of the albums and Christine might have come across it later. Lisa Walker could not explain why she had not bothered to sign her passport.

With reluctance, Lisa Walker decided to report the passport stolen. Police asked her not to discuss her missing passport with anyone else related to the case, particularly the Lamont family or Paul Joseph Gomez Mendes, whom Walker said she didn't know at all.

Paul Joseph Gomez Mendes got a phone call during his Christmas vacation in the sunny south of Portugal. A relative in Canada had read the newspaper accounts of the Brazilian kidnapping, including the fact that Mendes's name had come up as the false identity used by David Robert Spencer.

Paul Mendes had never heard of David Spencer, but mention of his co-accused, Christine Lamont, sent a worrisome chill down his spine — with good reason. Yes, he told his relatives, he knew Christine.

By the time his passport problems had made the evening news, Mendes was sitting as an elected member of the board of governors at Simon Fraser University and was just months away from graduation. He was also awaiting his acceptance into the prestigious University of Toronto Law School.

Within days of his return to Canada from his Christmas vacation, Mendes would also receive an unannounced, early-morning visit from RCMP officers. Mendes told them he had obtained a new passport the previous June and had lost it within days. He said he had last seen Christine Lamont around the same time that she had called him out of the blue and asked if they could meet at an East Vancouver café. Mendes told police that the two had met for coffee and Christine had told him that she had a friend in El Salvador who was in trouble and needed to get a Canadian passport to leave the country and escape the military death squads' campaign of terror. Mendes told police that he had refused Christine's request, telling her he needed his passport for an upcoming trip to Portugal. He said he put the incident out of his mind, even laughed it off, and invited Christine to a party he was having that weekend. Mendes's passport was in a briefcase in the bedroom of his apartment the night of the party, which Christine attended alone. It was later that week, he said, that he had noticed his passport was missing.

Mendes reported the document lost to the Vancouver RCMP detachment in the University of British Columbia campus district, which is not in the jurisdiction of the Vancouver city police. He was issued a second passport at the Vancouver passport office and left for Portugal within days of obtaining it. When the RCMP came calling after the passport turned up in Brazil, Mendes told police that he had never made any connection between Christine's asking him if she could have his passport and the document's disappearance.

Investigators found the young Mendes forthcoming and very willing to cooperate in any way to help them get to the bottom of their mystery. But it did not escape their attention that both Walker and Mendes had applied for their passports at the same Vancouver passport office on the same day, June 12.

Police found no trace of a criminal record for either Lamont or Spencer, although their outspoken activism on the streets of Vancouver meant that their faces were not unknown to West Coast police, who routinely monitored demonstrations, particularly after the Squamish Five bombings in the early 1980s. David Spencer's name turned up as one of the protesters outside the courthouse and as one of the visitors to the correctional facility in which some of the Squamish Five members were held.

Police continued their hunt for clues as to how this seemingly intelligent Canadian couple had met up with South American extremists with known ties to violent terrorist organizations throughout Latin America. Indeed, all but one of the eight people arrested with Christine and David had extensive criminal records.

The vital clue came to the RCMP, not from the Brazilian investigators piecing together the kidnappers' pasts, but from the mother of one of the Chileans arrested along with Christine and David.

Helena Urtubia, mother of Sergio Martin Olivares Urtubia, from San Felipe, Chile, contacted the Canadian consulate in São Paulo and said her son, one of the accused whom police had arrested and tortured in the hopes of being led to the house where Abílio Diniz was being held, was a Canadian citizen. Mrs. Urtubia was calling the consulate to demand Canadian intervention on her son's behalf. This information was passed along to the RCMP. Mrs.

Urtubia said her son had lived in Winnipeg with a woman, and that he had a Canadian-born son with the woman, who was by this time living in Saskatoon.

RCMP in Winnipeg traced Urtubia to an address just north of the city and, with information provided by Brazilian investigators, found Urtubia's Royal Bank branch. Transfer slips from the bank had been found in one of the six apartments rented by the kidnappers, which Brazilian police were systematically searching for evidence. At first, investigators assumed the bank slips belonged to the two Canadians, but with this new information from Mrs. Urtubia, they could then tie in Sergio Urtubia. From the bank, Urtubia's trail in Canada led to Vancouver, which made it possible for police to make a connection between him and Christine and David.

Police traced Urtubia's movements to the run-down bungalow in the city's east end, the house neighbours had referred to as a "Latin American flophouse," where they made the connection to Christine and David's circle of friends.

In fact, police in Canada reached even farther back and discovered that David and Urtubia had lived just blocks apart in Winnipeg, although they found no proof that the two had ever met in that city.

The report that Canadian authorities sent to their Brazilian counterparts was not the portrait of two seasoned terrorists, but it did provide the threads used to reinforce the web in which the two Canadians were hopelessly trapped.

CHAPTER 20

IN SEARCH OF ANSWERS

WHILE, IN CANADA, THE PIECES OF THE CASE WERE BEGINNING to come together, in Brazil, Keith and Marilyn's dreams and hopes for their daughter were falling apart.

The Lamonts' plane touched down in São Paulo early Thursday morning, December 21, just four days after the siege had ended at the house on Praca Hachiro Miyazaki. They went straight to the Canadian consulate in São Paulo, where they met Consul General William Ross and Pierre Pichette, who provided them with the latest news of Christine and David and a copy of the charges the pair faced. William Ross called the Avenida São Luiz offices of the Bandeira de Mello-Nahum e Advogados Associados. Their daughter's and David Spencer's lawyer, Marco Antonio Nahum, arranged to meet with the Lamonts first thing the next morning. Ross, who acted as the Lamonts' escort while they were in São Paulo, took them to their hotel and helped arrange for the Lamonts to have a thirty-minute visit with Christine behind the walls of the Penetenciaria Feminina do Estado the following afternoon. The couple emerged from their first meeting with their daughter with a prepared statement.

"We have come to see our daughter, who is in distress, and to give her whatever help and assistance we can," Keith told the throng of assembled reporters. "We found her to be in good condition, psychologically stable and unharmed." Despite previous arrangements with reporters to get some answers and report back as quickly as possible about their daughter's alleged involvement in the kidnapping, the Lamonts emerged tight-lipped about what Christine had had to say for herself during their meeting, except to report that she had requested cigarettes and English books to help pass the time in solitary confinement.

Whatever answers their daughter had given them during that emotion-filled first meeting, they were no longer willing to share them with the press. The Lamonts would dodge reporters for the remainder of their stay in Brazil. Notes left pinned to their hotel-room door at the São Paulo Marriott were not answered, nor were telephone messages left at the front desk. Amid all the confusion, and preoccupied with the seriousness of the situation, Keith and Marilyn decided that the reporters would have to wait.

During that first visit, Keith and Marilyn say that Christine whispered to them that they were not to discuss any events prior to her arrest for fear that their conversations were being monitored. They offered this information as an example of how her rights were being violated. But the Lamonts, with nothing to hide, might have wondered what it was about her activities that their daughter didn't want authorities to hear. What could Keith and Marilyn possibly say that would incriminate their daughter?

The Lamonts maintain that they didn't even ask Christine about the Diniz kidnapping during their first meetings with her in Brazil. Their only concern was for her safety and well-being. The details of the crime were of no consequence to them at that time. From the point of view of an outsider, it does seem odd that Keith and

Marilyn would board a plane for the long and expensive trip to São Paulo, meet with their daughter, and not ask why she was in Brazil in the first place, instead of Argentina where she was supposed to be on vacation, or Nicaragua where she was supposed to be working as a translator.

Over the few days after their first visit, the Lamonts saw Christine several times, including for a short period on Christmas day.

Keith said seeing his daughter alive and well was "the greatest Christmas present we could have had. We love her very much and that is why we are here. We hope things will turn out all right."

William Ross helped arrange for Keith and Marilyn to meet with the judge, to give them some sense of the judicial process awaiting Christine and David.

In Brazil, there are, in a sense, two different countries within the borders of one nation. There is the massive Third World nation filled with people who do not have enough to eat, people who live in shacks on the sides of the hills and children who live in gangs on the streets, stealing and begging for their survival. Then there is Brazil's First World, the world of racing-car drivers, polo championships, glamorous soap operas, and the jet set. This slice of Brazil comprises people who speak English fluently and who are university educated, many of them in the United States. These are the people behind Brazil's aerospace and high-technology industries, people who would be indistinguishable from their prosperous counterparts in North America or western Europe. These are the people who fill positions in government, the diplomatic corps, industry, and the judiciary.

Judge Barioni was of this First World. And, seen through the eyes of Brazilians, so were Keith and Marilyn Lamont. By virtue of their being Canadian, Christine and David had already been granted certain privileges. In Brazilian jails, inmates who are considered educated are given better prison cells, better food, better treatment. The two-tiered social structure of the nation is carried through the prison doors and is maintained inside the walled compounds. It is this distinction between rich and poor that had reassured Canadian consul Pierre Pichette that Christine and David were in no danger of being tortured after their arrest. The police in São Paulo knew full well that they were not dealing with Brazilian street thugs. They knew of the political reverberations that would come from torturing university-educated Canadians: it was never an option. The social structure was also the reason behind Keith and Marilyn's meeting with Judge Barioni. By virtue of their perceived upper-class status, they were granted a meeting with the man who would decide their daughter's fate. Barioni was anxious to meet the well-educated parents of one of the kidnappers who would appear before him within a matter of days. But the courtesy he was willing to extend to fellow members of the ruling class, be they Canadian or Brazilian, did not prevent him from telling them straight out that the situation did not look good for their daughter. As is typical in Brazil, Barioni was polite and gracious, but he chose his words carefully. He tried to be honest. He stated the obvious when he told Keith and Marilyn that he was under incredible pressure to convict all of the accused. But he also assured them that he was willing to give a fair hearing to each of the accused, their daughter included.

During their visits, Keith said Christine had been asking about David, whom she had not seen since their night together in the police station for questioning just after their arrest. Their daughter's concern about him led the Lamonts to arrange to see him.

The Lamonts waited until December 28 before getting permission to visit the unassuming-looking young man who had stolen their daughter's heart, and whose idealism may have cost her her freedom. They found David to be in good condition, quiet and characteristically calm. The visit, however, was a mistake. When they left, prison officials and prosecutors told them that, since they had met privately with one of the accused, they would not be allowed back in to see their daughter. Authorities wanted to prevent any possibility that the pair were collaborating on the stories they would later tell the judge. This was a rule that Christine and David's lawyers should have warned the Lamonts about. After two frustrating days of trying unsuccessfully to get permission to see Christine again, the Lamonts returned to Canada on New Year's Eve, leaving Christine alone in her dingy, stark jail cell just days before her trial was set to begin. They hadn't even said their good-byes.

As quickly as it had arisen, the story of Christine and David faded from Canadian media attention. Only scant details of their trial in early January were published. At this time, Keith and Marilyn started to make quiet inquiries about getting Christine home.

When news of the convictions came down in May, they felt that they had been betrayed by Judge Barioni. After he had been so kind to them during their meeting, the judge's decision came as a shock.

Details of the crime that emerged during the trial, including the houses the young couple had rented and the van David had brought in for repairs just days before the kidnapping, and the lies they told Barioni about their movements and false passports, did not find their way into the Canadian press. Consequently, people back home knew very little about the case — only what Keith and Marilyn were telling them.

Keith was fielding calls when news of the convictions reached Canada. He said the family was not taking the news well.

"They're really shocked and they think it's a long sentence for someone who is innocent," he said.

Keith and Marilyn took the obvious first steps after the convictions. They contacted the External Affairs department in Ottawa and began asking questions about how they could get Christine out, using diplomatic channels. For them it seemed so obvious: their daughter said she was innocent; Brazilian justice was not to be trusted by a First World nation like Canada; the Canadian government should therefore demand that its nationals be released immediately.

It was natural for the Lamonts to seek help from their own government. Canadians in trouble abroad often do so in the belief that there is something the diplomats in Ottawa can do to alter the justice system of another country. This is not the case. Canada's jurisdiction ends at the Canadian border. The rules which apply inside a Canadian courtroom cannot be transported to a developing nation half a world away. The Lamonts, like most Canadians, did not realize how powerless their own government was to intervene on behalf of Canadians in trouble abroad. In the coming months, they were going to be subjected to a harsh lesson in the reality of international relations.

The Lamonts say they tried to work quietly to pressure Ottawa to act in the early months after Christine and David were convicted. They met with staff at consular operations at External Affairs. Staff members reviewed the trial but felt there was nothing the department could do. There was no glaring instance of arbitrary detention. They had not been picked up off the street for questioning without just cause, but rather were caught in the same house as the victim, armed to the teeth, giving police more than enough reason to detain them. Ongoing appeals in the Brazilian courts meant the case was far from over, and Canada's policy of non-interference in the judicial system of another nation was firm.

In Brazil, representatives from the consulate in São Paulo still visited regularly with the two Canadians. The case took up much of William Ross's time in Brazil. He worked to establish a relationship with the wardens of the huge jail compound on the outskirts of the sprawling city in which Christine and David were being held. He had access to prison directors whenever he had any questions about medical treatment or prison conditions in general. He ensured that the Canadians were also visited by a Canadian doctor attached to the consulate.

But as far as Keith and Marilyn were concerned, nothing was really being done to help their daughter, to bring her home from a place in which she did not belong.

In the early months of 1991, after several visits to see Christine in prison, the Lamonts geared up to demand more than consular visits from the External Affairs department. They had collected legal opinions and had uncovered a provision in Brazilian law that allowed for the outright expulsion of foreigners from the country. Expulsion could be granted under the sole authority of the president of Brazil after a high-level, state-to-state request from Ottawa. If granted, the subjects would be expelled from Brazil, free to go wherever they pleased. For Keith and Marilyn Lamont, this looked like the salvation they had been hoping for, a chance to have Christine come home a free woman. All Ottawa, specifically External Affairs minister Joe Clark, had to do was ask Brazil to send the couple home. They could not come up with a single reason why the Canadian government wouldn't agree.

It was during this time in early 1991 that Keith and Marilyn Lamont were introduced to David Humphreys, a relative of a friend of theirs. David Humphreys owned the Humphreys Public Affairs Group, based in Ottawa. The company did public relations and lobbying, and offered a media-monitoring service. Humphreys himself was a former Ottawa bureau chief for *The Globe and Mail* and former managing editor of *The Ottawa Journal*. He was one of the better-connected people in the capital.

One of Humphreys's connections during the life of Brian Mulroney's Conservative government was his decades-old friendship with Joe Clark. Humphreys and Clark first met in the summer of 1958 when Humphreys was a reporter for *The Edmonton Journal* and Clark arrived as a summer student. They crossed paths again as editors of university papers. Humphreys edited *The Manitoban* in 1959–60 at the University of Manitoba. That same year Joe Clark edited the University of Alberta's student paper, *The*

Gateway. Their friendship continued through the years as Clark made a name for himself in the Progressive Conservative party and Humphreys worked his way up as a newspaperman, lending his younger friend cash if he needed it for his cross-country campaigning treks in the early 1960s. In 1965, as managing editor of the morning paper *The Albertan*, Humphreys gave Clark a summer job as a reporter so that the young politician could be closer to Peter Lougheed, who had just been elected as provincial party leader.

Clark found an open door and free room with Humphreys and his wife while the senior journalist was working in London, England, for FP Publications. As Clark rose to become an MP, and later Tory leader, and, for a short nine months, Prime Minister of Canada in a minority government before being pushed from office by a vote of non-confidence, he maintained his close friendship with David Humphreys. It was during Clark's early days as Leader of Her Majesty's Loyal Opposition that David Humphreys wrote the book *Joe Clark: A Portrait*, an account of his friend's historic rise in Canadian politics. It was published in 1978.

If there was one man in Ottawa whom Keith and Marilyn needed to help them get the ear of the Secretary of State for External Affairs, it was David L. Humphreys. If there was anyone who might be able to pull some strings, and put a sympathetic twist on their daughter's plight, it was Humphreys. He knew Ottawa, he knew the system, and he knew the man who counted the most in the Lamonts' quest to free their daughter. Despite all of this, Humphreys wasn't enough.

It is unknown whether Humphreys was paid from the very beginning or if he volunteered his services at first, then went on to work formally for the Lamonts as their struggle dragged on and turned uphill.

Officials in the Department of External Affairs had reviewed the case at the Lamonts' request and concluded that, in the absence of any serious miscarriage of justice worthy of Canadian interference, there was nothing they could do to help. Joe Clark accordingly refused a request to meet with the Lamonts to discuss Christine's character, her commitment to being a vegetarian, and her life-long history of non-violence, which her family continued to point to as proof that she must be innocent of the kidnapping charges.

In Ottawa, time was running out for David Humphreys to help the Lamonts get Joe Clark to change his mind, using press kits and detailing the injustice of their imprisonment to his old friend as part of his lobbying technique. A Cabinet shuffle was imminent, and soon his well-placed connection and old friend would be moved to another post. Humphreys would later tell supporters of Christine and David that he honestly felt they were making serious headway towards gaining the pair's release when Clark was minister in those early days of 1991. But, in early April 1991, Joe Clark became National Unity minister, called upon by his old adversary Prime Minister Brian Mulroney to piece Canada together and come up with a formula for national unity that would be both acceptable and lasting. Clark took up the challenge — some say reluctantly — and left the high-profile position at External Affairs to Barbara McDougall, former Employment and Immigration minister and the highest-ranking woman in the Mulroney government, whose name was already being mentioned as a possible successor to the prime minister.

With this less than encouraging news, the Lamonts now turned all their energies towards convincing the new minister that theirs was a story worth listening to and acting upon.

CHAPTER 21

FINDING FRIENDS

BARBARA MCDOUGALL FIRST HEARD ABOUT CHRISTINE AND David's case as part of a larger, more general briefing on consular services just days after she took over the office of Secretary of State for External Affairs in May 1991.

"There was a suggestion that the Lamonts had tried to put some pressure on Joe [Clark]. Joe would not see them. I did feel some sympathy for the parents and as an issue it would kind of come and go," McDougall remembers.

McDougall, perhaps unfairly, was not widely considered one of the warmest people in Canadian politics. Despite her immediate scrutiny of the case and her directive to staff to look at Christine and David's situation once again, she was almost immediately perceived by Keith and Marilyn as the only obstacle keeping Christine and David in Brazil, jailed in unsanitary, life-threatening conditions.

McDougall says that, despite her image, she was not as unyielding as people thought. She was used to listening to people as they pitched for a second chance, a second glance at their file, another opportunity to be heard: "Having dealt with immigration [her previous portfolio], I always felt every human being has a story to tell. You're saying no to a lot of people in that job and it has an impact on a lot of lives."

She said she was willing to give Christine and David's case a great deal of her attention, and was prepared to listen to the Lamonts when they first made their desire for an expulsion request known.

"I looked at it exhaustively and there was nothing to lead me to believe in their innocence, there was just nothing there for us to grab onto. But I wasn't going to back off seeing them," she said.

By the summer of 1991, McDougall had already informed the Lamonts that she had reviewed the case and could not see any justification for an expulsion request. The Lamonts, increasingly desperate more than a year and a half after Christine's arrest, once again sought the assistance of David Humphreys, who looked for help elsewhere on Parliament Hill. The first place the Lamonts took their plea was the most obvious: the opposition. Liberal External Affairs critic Lloyd Axworthy and his New Democratic Party counterpart Svend Robinson were contacted and "briefed" on the situation. Both were faxed copies of the Lamonts' early statements. These were rambling, lengthy accounts of what they called the "injustices" in the "alleged" kidnapping case against their daughter. Those same statements sent to politicians across Canada rehashed some, but not all, of the evidence presented at the trial. Notably missing was the information about the two houses they had modified and details of their duplicate passports and of David's involvement in preparing the van that was used in the crime. The false passports, an important part of the original stories that ran in Canada about Christine and David, faded from the spotlight and were never resurrected by the Lamonts.

"Using a false passport is a crime in every country in the world. The Lamonts just didn't want to talk about that," remembers McDougall.

To refute the eye-witness testimony that said Christine and David handled weapons during the siege, the Lamonts replied: "Neither of them had either loaded or fired a gun — in fact, it is unlikely that either had ever handled a gun before the house was surrounded by heavily armed police." No credence was given to Abílio Diniz's statement to police and friends that he had never seen a woman who could handle a gun like Christine Lamont could. As time passed, the Lamonts would say that piece of information was a mistake in translation, and Diniz actually was referring to Christine's obvious inexperience with a weapon. Everyone who heard the man utter the words feels differently. "He meant it exactly the way he said, exactly the way it was interpreted, that she knew only too well what she was doing," said a Canadian RCMP officer working in Brazil at the time of the arrests.

The Lamonts' initial "information kits," which hummed off fax machines in politicians' offices across the country, reminded would-be supporters again and again that their daughter was "a caring, loving and basically humanitarian type of person since an early age. As a child she initiated a group to 'adopt' an indigent child living in India — sending money and goods on a regular basis for several years. She has been a vegetarian for twelve years, not because of health theories about meat, but because she disapproved of killing of animals for her own use."

The war of words which the Lamonts had embarked on knew no limits. The paper trail from their house to Parliament Hill grew daily, and regular updates and dispatches from Brazil were constantly finding their way to Ottawa.

On November 19, 1991, just a month shy of Christine and David's second anniversary in prison, McDougall appeared before the Parliamentary Committee of External Affairs and International Trade, on which both Lloyd Axworthy and Svend Robinson sat. The previous week, both Opposition politicians had met separately in Vancouver with Keith and Marilyn. When the committee sat,

Axworthy was the first to chastise McDougall on her stance.

"For the life of me, I do not understand why you and your department refused to take any action whatsoever to ask for the expulsion of these Canadians by the Brazilian officials and to gain for them their proper rights and proper treatment. They are being treated abominably," he said.

McDougall stood by her decision: "I am satisfied that there is not an absence of justice or any irregularities. There are no humanitarian or compassionate grounds on which to initiate an approach to the Brazilian government for the expulsion of the prisoners."

Axworthy had barely finished his questioning when Svend Robinson took up the cause: "The minister has said that she has acted on behalf of these people, that her ministry has acted on their behalf, but I want to tell the minister that the families are feeling a tremendous sense of betrayal and anger that their government has not done more in these circumstances, that they are particularly incensed at the suggestion that there have been no miscarriages of justice, no irregularities."

Robinson went on to urge McDougall to reconsider her decision in light of the legal reports that the family had paid lawyers in Toronto to produce after reviewing the case. McDougall said her department had an open mind about the case and was willing to consider new evidence as it came in. But McDougall reminded the committee that Canada, as a signatory to the International Convention Against the Taking of Hostages, stood to lose the respect of other nations and a healthy dose of its international prestige if it then asked that two convicted kidnappers walk free on Canadian soil.

To this comment by McDougall, Keith Lamont objected.

"We take issue with the premise that expulsion equates with either clemency or pardon," he said, leaving officials in Ottawa wondering what it did mean if a person convicted of a crime was released unconditionally from prison before serving out his or her sentence and allowed to return to Canada, without so much as a criminal record. The Lamonts went on to announce that they wished "to express our outrage and disgust that External Affairs minister Barbara McDougall has chosen to play politics with our children's lives."

It was amid this furore that news of the longer, twenty-eight-year sentences had reached the parents. Although perhaps less shocking than the news of the arrests delivered by phone on December 17, 1989, this news was much grimmer.

The Lamonts were the first to recover and attempt to turn the lengthy terms to their daughter's favour.

"Our first reaction was that this is very bad news, devastating," Marilyn told the reporters who phoned and were put through to her by a secretary at her Langley home. "But we've had time to think about it, and now we see that maybe it could turn out to be helpful, because what it demonstrates is that you can't possibly look to Brazil for justice."

Barbara McDougall responded to the new sentences by directing her ambassador in Brasilia to express Canada's concern over their severity, but she made no offer to reconsider her rejection of the expulsion request.

Just three weeks after her appearance before the parliamentary committee, with feelings running high, Keith and Marilyn, along with Bill Spencer and David's sister Judy Hartling, met Barbara McDougall for the first time.

"It wasn't a happy meeting," remembers McDougall. "They were very tense, particularly Mrs. Lamont. They were not interested in a discussion. There was one thing they wanted: their kids — and they are not kids — to come home free and clear. And with all the goodwill in the world, if I'd bought everything they said, it [expulsion] still wasn't going to happen."

Before Christine and David were arrested, officials at External Affairs had been exploring the possibility of having in place a Transfer of Offenders Treaty with Brazil. The South American country had been a haven for criminals from the world over. People like Ronald Biggs, one of the thirteen men who took part in Britain's Great Train Robbery in 1963, made off from Scotland with $2.6 million and resurfaced in 1974 living in the luxury of Brazil's First World. British authorities were unsuccessful in getting Brazil to ship Biggs back to prison because by then he had a Brazilian-born son. It would be a diplomatic feather in Canada's cap to negotiate successfully a treaty with Brazil. It would also provide a viable method to bring Christine and David home, although they would not walk away free, but rather would have to serve their sentences in Canada. Nonetheless, once home, they would be eligible for parole, something they were not entitled to as foreigners jailed in Brazil.

But despite attempts by staff at External Affairs to discuss the ongoing treaty negotiations with the Lamonts, they didn't want to hear it.

"They refused to even listen to the progress my department was making," said McDougall. "It was expulsion or nothing."

McDougall said she was assured by her department, which had made discreet inquiries in Brazil about the true nature of expulsion requests, that the Lamonts were being simplistic in thinking she could wave a magic wand and influence the president of Brazil. "It wasn't going to happen; there was no chance those two were going to walk free, even if I had believed there were grounds for the request, which I didn't. I had nothing I could even take to an international court, not with the evidence used to convict them being so strong."

Much later, McDougall would point to the 1994 case of an American teenager who was sentenced to be caned in a Singapore jail for spray-painting cars in an act of vandalism. Appeals by eighteen-year-old Michael Fay's family resulted in his caning being reduced from six lashes to four, but still the punishment was meted out, over the objections of U.S. president Bill Clinton.

"If the President of the United States did not have the power to stop something like that, what makes people think that the External Affairs minister of Canada had the power to get two convicted terrorists released unconditionally?" asked McDougall. "You just cannot tell another country what to do, it doesn't work."

When the meeting between McDougall and the families was over, the minister had other business to attend to. The aftermath of the war in the Persian Gulf still demanded a great deal of her time in her new portfolio. Christine and David's case continued to surface periodically, and McDougall said it took up a great deal of her staff's time. But, she insists, consular staff never begrudged the visits to check on their well-being, to ensure they were receiving any supplies they needed, to give them news of Canada and relay any messages home. "That's a big part of the job," said McDougall. The same cannot be said, however, for the amount of time that Christine's parents occupied: "They were really quite abusive to my staff, both on the phone and in person."

McDougall would quietly tolerate the constant barrage of criticism levelled at her by the Lamonts, but the day would come when she could say "Enough." The day would come when the Lamonts would push too hard.

CHAPTER 22

IN GOD WE TRUST

THE LAMONTS' EARLY ATTEMPTS AT PUBLIC RELATIONS IN THE first half of 1991 fell victim to the overwhelming publicity surrounding the Persian Gulf War. The plight of their daughter and her fiancé was overshadowed by a bigger story in another hemisphere.

After the war and its aftermath, the story of Christine Lamont and David Spencer was old news, and the Canadian media found little reason to resurrect it. Then, late in 1991, the war of words between the Lamonts and External Affairs began to be played out in West Coast newspapers. Whenever External Affairs reiterated that they could not justify asking for expulsion, the Lamonts were quoted as feeling betrayed by their government.

"This has been a lesson to us to find out where the government's allegiance is," Keith told a Vancouver paper. "It certainly isn't to its own citizens."

After their Ottawa meeting with Barbara McDougall, the all-out media campaign began in earnest.

The decision to launch a massive media campaign is not an easy one to make. There are consequences: campaigners may find that their privacy is invaded; they will have to endure mind-numbing repetition as reporters ask the same questions over and over again; and the cost involved is not inconsiderable. But, by this point, Keith and Marilyn could not turn back. They were convinced of Christine's innocence and committed to gaining her freedom. For more than two years they had been making sacrifices. Both their time and their money had been eaten up as they installed computers and fax machines in their basement; hired office staff to deal with the mail and telephone calls; and paid for lobbyists in Ottawa, lawyers in Toronto, and more lawyers in São Paulo. A media-monitoring service on the west coast would later be added to the list of organizations inadvertently benefiting from one family's tragedy. There seemed to be no end to the bills to pay for their campaign.

As time passed, the answers to reporters' questions took on a professional, polished quality. Perhaps without realizing what was happening to them, Keith and Marilyn were becoming skilled manipulators of the media. Their rambling press releases were replaced by short, snappy accusations, complete with headlines to grab the reader's eye. The entire case-history was turned into a "one-page summary," which again omitted any mention of false passports. At every turn, Keith and Marilyn made it clear to officials in Ottawa and anyone else who was listening that they would not be stopped.

A 1992 letter to then Justice minister Kim Campbell captures the mood in the Lamont home. It reads: "We assure you that we are not going away until justice is done. We are totally convinced that we are right, that the public is overwhelmingly on our side, and that External Affairs position is untenable. An advertisement in *The Globe and Mail* which is our next step will appear shortly. We appeal to you as Justice Minister and as the political minister for British Columbia to use your influence to see that justice is done."

Calls to the Lamont home were always answered by efficient

help and were returned within an hour; even when Keith and Marilyn were out of the country they saw to it that they were never out of touch. They had concluded that their real chances for success, for getting the expulsion order they so desired, was by garnering support in the media, specifically, the national media. They never strayed from the course that had been decided upon, and their story began to stick. It went like this: Christine and David were innocent dupes. They did not know that Abílio Diniz was being held in the house they rented. They did not know their roommates were a gang of international terrorists. They didn't know that a cell had been constructed underneath the kitchen of the house they had rented. They did not know there was a cache of arms, including submachine-guns, in their house. They were in Brazil doing unspecified human-rights work with unspecified others. Yes, the Lamonts knew this sounded a bit hard to believe, but they also knew Canadians to be "fair-minded people" who would be willing to give Christine and David the benefit of the doubt.

In early 1992, God was added to the growing list of Lamont/Spencer supporters.

Through churches across the country, the Lamonts could reach out to tens of thousands of Canadians who could help them convince Ottawa of their daughter's innocence. Churchgoers could also prove to be a political force to be reckoned with, and the Lamonts were hopeful that Conservative politicians in Ottawa would see the will of conservative Canadians — Canadians who tended to cast Tory votes.

Reverend Douglas Brown first met Keith and Marilyn Lamont in the early 1960s when he was the local United Church minister in Fort St. John, in the northern interior of British Columbia. Keith Lamont, just returned from the United States with his young family, was the general surgeon in the local hospital. The Browns and Lamonts became fast and lasting friends; even after Reverend Brown and his wife had moved to the Toronto area and the Lamonts had relocated to Langley, B.C., the two couples kept in touch.

When Doug Brown saw the front page of *The Toronto Star* on December 19, 1989, featuring a picture of Christine Lamont shackled to her boyfriend in a São Paulo police station, he picked up the phone and dialled Keith and Marilyn's number in Langley to offer his support and ask if there was anything he could do. At that point, the Lamonts didn't know what they were dealing with and could only thank Reverend Brown for his concern and promise to keep him up-to-date on what was happening. As the months passed and Christine's plight worsened, culminating in the twenty-eight-year prison term, Doug Brown geared up to ask for favours and rally support for Christine and David back home, in the hopes of pressuring the Canadian government to act on their behalf. He made the decision to get deeply involved in the struggle to free Christine and David on the basis of his relationship with her parents. Like so many other supporters, he became committed to working on behalf of Christine and David because of the integrity and honesty of Keith and Marilyn Lamont. Revered Brown had not seen Christine since she was a child in Sunday school.

The Lamonts' commitment to their daughter made them magnets for concerned Canadians, people with families of their own, people who could identify with them. Marilyn, on radio shows and in interviews, would remind people that "our family really isn't very different from yours." Her message struck a chord. Marilyn spent months travelling the country, appearing at church-organized rallies in Toronto and Ottawa in hopes of raising the profile of her daughter's case. She is a well-spoken woman who makes no effort to hide her overwhelming love for Christine. She is easy to like and easy to believe. The reason her version of the events leading up to her daughter's imprisonment is so easy to swallow, despite the mass of evidence used to convict the pair, is that she firmly believes every word she speaks. She is not putting on a show for the cameras; she is telling it as she sees it. Many disappointed supporters would realize too late that Marilyn Lamont sees things through the eyes of a woman devoted to gaining her child's freedom at any price.

It was the first week of March 1992 when Reverend Brown dropped by the Toronto headquarters of the United Church of Canada Division of Mission offices on St. Clair Avenue East with a file on Christine and David. The file contained a few newspaper clippings, including *Vancouver Sun* stories written from São Paulo that proclaimed Lamont and Spencer to be innocent dupes of a sinister kidnapping plot by seasoned terrorists. What Reverend Brown did not know was that an employee with the United Church used to work for External Affairs and was able to make some discreet inquiries about the Lamont/Spencer case to help the church decide on the direction to take. Reverend Brown requested a letter from the Moderator of the United Church to Barbara McDougall asking that the Canadian government seek the pair's expulsion. The request stated that Reverend Brown had known Christine as a child, when her parents were members of his church in Fort St. John. It didn't say when Reverend Brown had last seen Christine, who was now approaching her thirty-third birthday. After a review of the case, the church decided that it was not in a position to judge the merits of the case or the equity of the criminal-justice system in Brazil. Inquiries in Ottawa revealed that there was no documented case of the Brazilian president signing an expulsion request from another nation to repatriate convicted criminals. The church concluded that the best approach was to send a letter to McDougall expressing pastoral concern and asking that she continue to pursue every available avenue to ensure that these two Canadians were being treated fairly in Brazil. The letter was signed by General Secretary Reverend Dr. Howie Mills and sent to McDougall within days of the receipt of Reverend Brown's request. A copy of the letter was then sent to Brown, who in turn faxed it to Keith and

Marilyn, and to David Humphreys in Ottawa to keep him abreast of any developments or shows of support.

The letter was not what Reverend Brown and the Lamonts had hoped for. It was not a strongly worded demand for action, but rather a polite inquiry. In a follow-up note, Reverend Brown asked that the church change the wording in a future letter to ask specifically for an expulsion request instead of "relying on uncertain appeals process." The United Church, in pursuing a conservative approach to the case, did not want to delve blindly into a situation it knew little about. Publicity surrounding the case was growing, and the Canadian Broadcasting Corporation's *fifth estate* was due to broadcast a segment on Christine and David that same week. As an adviser noted in a memo to the Moderator, Reverend Dr. Mills, " 'fifth estate' is doing a piece on this case tonight. That won't affect the decision of the government, but it may well affect us. People in Toronto West Presbytery have already been alerted to this case. The UCC [United Church of Canada] connection is likely to become known." Church officials knew that they had to tread carefully. They were well aware of their own power and influence, and they went to great lengths not to abuse that influence in a case whose merits were, at best, doubtful. It was hard to overlook the problem of the false passports and the fact that Christine and David had been caught in the same house as the kidnapping victim. No matter how kind Keith and Marilyn were, and how close they were to their daughter's childhood minister, the church's senior members knew enough about human nature to think twice before jumping to Christine and David's unconditional defence. Reverend Brown would be disappointed by his church's inaction and would fight on for Christine and David's release at the local presbytery level.

That edition of *fifth estate*, which ran the day the church sent its letter to McDougall, gave Canadians their first look at Christine and David, interviewed separately behind the bars of their São Paulo jails. Both came across as intelligent, determined, and confident that they had done nothing wrong. They did not express regret for cheapening the much-respected Canadian passport by using false identities, and they didn't appear outraged at having been effectively tricked by ringleader Humberto Paz into becoming involved in the kidnapping. Canadians heard from Christine the reasoning behind using the phoney passports. She said it was really quite simple: "Go on another passport, keep your own. If there's ever any problem, you have your own passport ready and you can leave the country without problem. . . . It's true we were breaking the law, and what we were doing also was protecting ourselves." Lamont said the pair travelled on false passports on the advice of other human-rights workers, who suggested it was an easy way to escape a dangerous government in a part of the world where democracy was still in its infancy and the idea of human rights was nowhere near the forefront of people's minds.

Fifth estate also featured an interview with Keith and Marilyn. Keith tells the interviewer that all it would take to bring Christine and David home was "a simple request to the department of foreign affairs in Brazil. A two-sentence request would do it — two sentences." On a trip to Brazil to visit Christine in January, the Lamonts had met with Brazil's minister of Justice, Jarba Passarinho, to whom they appealed for mercy on their daughter's behalf. Passarinho, a seasoned politician and good friend of President Fernando Collor de Mello, had diplomatically told the Lamonts that "for anguished parents, anything is possible" and told them to urge their government to make the expulsion request, which is what they had been doing for months on end. He did not vow to send Christine and David home, he did not say they were innocent, he did not say that his friend the president would agree. He made his suggestions to assuage the fears and worries of panicked parents whom he had agreed to meet as a favour to Archbishop Dom Paulo Evaristo Cardinal Arns. Political observers in Brazil say Passarinho is far too astute a tactician to promise, or even suggest to his colleagues in government, that convicted terrorists be set free, especially terrorists whose capture was seen as a political coup for the right wing.

The Lamonts interpreted the meeting to be a commitment to free their daughter as soon as Canada made the request.

It all sounded so easy. Reverend Brown thought it was that easy, and that's the message he passed along to congregation members when he asked them to write to Ottawa and demand action and mercy for Christine and David. In the months to come, Brown's message would reach thousands of other church members through council meetings and friendship with others involved in the church. The circle of supporters was growing by the week, and the flood of mail into Ottawa was being noticed by senior ministry officials and Barbara McDougall herself.

CHAPTER 23

FIGHTING BACK

ONE OF THE THOUSANDS OF LETTERS INQUIRING ABOUT CHRISTINE and David had a return address in Shelbourne, Ontario, a small town two hours' drive northwest of Toronto. It came from Mrs. Verna Carruthers, housewife, mother of four, local volunteer. Mrs. Carruthers did not write to demand that Christine and David be set free, that the government intervene immediately on their behalf. Instead, she wrote a polite inquiry to her MP, then Communications minister Perrin Beatty, requesting any available information about the Lamont/Spencer case.

Christine and David's struggle reached Verna Carruthers via her local United Church, where she attended a meeting of the church's women's committee in 1992. Members were asked to participate in the campaign to free Christine and David. A leader with the church had attended a conference at which Reverend Doug Brown had given a presentation on Christine and David and attempted to drum up support. That message was then brought back to congregations across Ontario. Verna Carruthers was exactly the sort of person the campaign was looking for. Though separated from her by thousands of kilometres, she was not unlike Marilyn Lamont, a mother and grandmother in a family with a higher-than-average income, a woman committed to raising her children, a woman who went to church and remained active in her community. Verna was exactly what the campaign needed — women with time on their hands to commit to the cause, women who could identify with the tragedy that had struck the Lamont family. But Verna Carruthers is also a woman who knows how to ask a few questions.

"I just don't believe that you run into something without checking on the facts," said Verna. "I don't lobby government without knowing exactly what I'm talking about."

Verna knew Perrin Beatty through various local activities, including the Rotary Club. He referred her letter to a colleague at External Affairs who in turn sent a thick package through the mail slot of the Carruthers' large brick, farmhouse-style home. The contents of the envelope made one thing perfectly clear: after months of being portrayed as the enemy of Canada and of young Canadians in trouble, Barbara McDougall had decided to fight back.

McDougall had authorized her staff to release copies of an internal investigation that she had ordered after the Lamonts' Canadian lawyers presented her and her staff with a lengthy report detailing irregularities in the trial of Christine and David and outlining reasons why their convictions should not be an obstacle to Canada's deciding to request their freedom. The point had come when the Lamonts had pushed McDougall too far.

"Somebody had to say, enough already; it was getting ridiculous. They had every church in the country wrapped around their little finger; it just wasn't right," said McDougall in explaining her decision. She said the constant pressure in Ottawa, the flood of letters, the growing protests by people who didn't know the details of the case — all became too much.

The Lamonts had even tried to bring the prime minister onside when they crashed a Conservative party fund-raiser in downtown Vancouver on December 3, 1991. They cornered Brian Mulroney's wife, Mila, at the event. After hearing the Lamonts' tale, the elegant and glamorous wife of the prime minister, herself a mother of four, had called her husband over to meet the Lamonts. In a quick exchange, Mulroney agreed to look into the matter in the near future, before the Lamonts were ushered from the ballroom, leaving a reportedly furious prime minister questioning security at the $250-a-plate event. The Lamonts may have been winning the public-relations battle, but they were not winning friends in Ottawa's corridors of power.

As Verna Carruthers would soon learn, as would thousands of others across the country who had sent letters of inquiry or complaint to Ottawa, the picture wasn't quite as Keith and Marilyn Lamont, with the help of David Humphreys, had painted it.

The seventeen-page report detailed the case in Brazil against the Canadians and concluded that there was enough evidence for a conviction, even if Canadian law had been applied. For the first time, in many cases, would-be supporters learned of the inconsistencies in the testimony given by Christine and David, of the lies about how and where they had obtained false passports, of the information about their actions leading up to the kidnapping, including the renting and modifying of two houses in preparation for the arrival of the victim.

When she decided to make the report public, McDougall sent a note to the Lamonts, stating that, given the amount of interest in the case, she thought it would be best to have the conclusions of her department out in the open. Up until this point, the External Affairs department had toed the privacy line, a convenient and often-employed tool of the Mulroney government that covered much of what the government was doing in a blanket of secrecy. The vaguely worded Access to Information Act, first introduced in 1983, sent a message to bureaucrats in Ottawa that privacy was the order of the day and information was to be handed out sparingly. It was invoked often during the first two years of Lamont and Spencer's incarceration.

In response to the barrage of criticism coming from the Lamonts, employees at External Affairs could offer up no explanations, no details, and no reasons for the government's actions or decision not to intervene beyond the consular visits and any required medical help. All they could say in a standard form letter was that everything possible was being done for the pair.

With the release of the report, which found its way first to some West-Coast media that had been especially supportive of the Lamonts' campaign, the secrecy was gone, and Barbara McDougall hoped the facts as released would put an end, once and for all, to the Lamonts' campaign.

For Verna Carruthers, it was more than enough to convince anyone of the pair's guilt. It also angered her that she had been misled by her church. Although the United Church had never formally endorsed the campaign or Reverend Brown's work on Christine and David's behalf, the perception by congregation members was that their church leaders were asking for their help. For Verna Carruthers and others like her across Canada, the report triggered an angry reaction that had church leaders backpedalling from their commitment to help and vowing to be increasingly wary of requests in the future.

But with their media machine in full swing, the Lamonts were distraught but not swayed by the release of the report. They fought on. Within five days they had prepared a response to the minister's report, which was written with the help of one of their lawyers, Queen's University law professor Jennie Hatfield-Lyon.

As a prime example of the growing tendency in the Lamont camp to weight the information in their favour, Hatfield-Lyon's memo to the Lamonts attempts to counter the report's conclusion that there was nothing to indicate that Judge Barioni had not acted impartially. The report stated that the judge's own admission that he was under a great deal of pressure to convict indicated that he was willing to rise above that pressure and hold a fair hearing. To counter this point, Hatfield-Lyon pointed out that the judge had admitted to the CBC's *fifth estate* that "it is possible that Christine and David are innocent." Anyone who had not seen the program would have accepted Hatfield-Lyon's apparently direct quotation from the taped interview without question. But that is not what Judge Barioni said in the interview. The question put to the judge was whether or not it was possible that Christine and David were innocent. The judge replied: "It is possible because everything is possible — but they don't convince me." The memo was just one more example of how the Lamont supporters seemed to see and hear only what they wanted to. The tone of Barioni's interview made it clear that he did not think he had made a mistake, that he was convinced of their guilt and convicted them accordingly.

In their formal press release, issued seven days after McDougall's report, the Lamonts attempted to counter several other points it had raised, points they referred to as part of a "smear campaign." Their response to the testimony that placed Christine and David in their first rented house, where they modified the entrance and barred the windows with wood, and to other witnesses' reports that placed David at the garage where the van had been taken for repairs, was that "witnesses have been known to be bribed and intimidated." There was no evidence that this had happened. Years later, the witnesses stick to the stories they told to the judge directly or in signed affidavits. No witness has changed his mind. No one has recanted testimony.

In response to the information about the renting of the first house on Rúa Pugliesi, the Lamonts wrote: "Re: the reason for abandoning the Pugliesi house. The police claim it was across the street from a police officer's residence. If David were aware of plans to kidnap, would he be likely to make such a mistake? If he did make a mistake, how long would it take him to correct it?"

This argument portrays David as astute and incapable of making a stupid mistake. Yet, Canadians were also supposed to believe that he didn't know anything about the kidnapping, he had been duped, he was naïve. The Lamonts' explanation gives no reason for David's decision to lie about the house in court. The press release goes on: "Re: the alleged statement that a neighbour living near this house said that Christine said that they were leaving because her mother in Holland had cancer — she simply did not say that." Yet that woman, who still lives down the street, continues to be convinced that "Lisa" told her just that. "Why would I lie? I have nothing to hide, I didn't kidnap anybody," said the woman in an interview. To instances in which Christine and David's testimony was contradictory, the Lamont press release responds simply: "They got their signals crossed."

The undiminished determination by the Lamonts to rescue their daughter had its effect, and the McDougall report was soon forgotten. Details of the report received very little media attention, the press bowing to its love of a heart-breaking story over a merely factual one. Those reporters who had climbed on the "free Christine and David" bandwagon were not about to jump off just months later. Neither were the politicians.

CHAPTER 24

REASONABLE EXPLANATIONS

IN THE BRITISH COLUMBIA CONSTITUENCY OFFICE OF FRASER Valley West Conservative MP Bob Wenman, staff came to expect a particular phone call every morning. Every morning, Marilyn Lamont was on the other end of the line, asking for updates, questioning Wenman, keeping up the pressure. Campaign workers for the long-time MP remember being told in no uncertain terms that, if Wenman didn't stand up in caucus in Ottawa and demand that Barbara McDougall reverse her position on the expulsion request, the Lamonts, along with their friends and supporters, would work tirelessly to ensure that the next federal election marked the end of his political career. Wenman had held his riding since 1974 — it was considered to be the safest Tory seat in the province. But there was little Wenman could do as a back-bencher. Other B.C. politicians, such as Surrey–White Rock–South Langley's Benno Friesen, McDougall's parliamentary secretary, refused to be swayed by the threats from Lamont and Spencer supporters and backed McDougall's stance on the case completely.

Still, with the bills for their efforts mounting daily, the Lamonts continued to push. With every passing week, in every media interview, their desperation mounted. In Ottawa, David Humphreys pushed for hearings in front of the Parliamentary Committee on External Affairs and International Trade. The chairman, John Bosley, refused to hear the case. Humphreys then tried Justice, and the Chairman of the Standing Committee on Justice and the Solicitor General, Dr. Bob Horner, a hard-working back-bencher who represented the Mississauga West riding, a sprawling Toronto suburb. Horner had first heard about the case from Tory Alberta back-bencher Blaine Thacker, who also sat on Horner's committee. The Justice committee was not the appropriate place for hearings into Christine and David's case. The committee dealt with domestic issues of crime and punishment and heard opinions on new security measures being taken and the like. But, in Bob Horner, David Humphreys found a sympathetic listener, and the Lamonts found a new spokesperson through whom they could get their message out. In Bob Horner, Barbara McDougall found a new headache.

Like so many of their supporters, Bob Horner was an older man, not too many years away from retirement. He had led a very comfortable life and had a successful career as an equine veterinarian. He is a man who is comfortable around the racetrack and has a large, comfortable home complete with toys on hand for visiting grandchildren. Like the Lamonts, the Horners had four children.

"I got to know the parents, and being a parent myself of four kids, about the same age as Christine and David, and knowing how they sort of were drawn to radicalism and the left wing, I felt a lot of empathy for their situation," said Horner, who laughs when he tells the story of his son canvassing for the New Democratic Party at the same time his father was running for the federal Tories. "My son the pinko! Can you believe that one?"

In this politician, Keith and Marilyn had tapped into the very root of their support. Luckily for them, they had found him well positioned and respected — on Parliament Hill.

"The family are truly fine people, and I guess to do what they have done they have to be convinced of the innocence of Christine," said Horner.

In making his decision to hold hearings in the late spring of 1992, Horner said he was influenced by the feeling that officials in External Affairs were not telling everything they knew, that they had additional information that was influencing their decision not to seek expulsion. From what he had seen in the Lamonts' "briefs," he felt Christine and David had probably already paid a hefty price for their involvement.

When the hearings were announced, more than a few of Horner's Tory colleagues chastised him for going against Barbara McDougall's wishes. "I got a few cold stares in those days."

The Lamonts, along with Bill Spencer, spent weeks in preparation. Their two Brazilian lawyers, Marco Antonio Nahum and Belisario dos Santos, were flown up from São Paulo to help convince the committee to push the minister to ask for expulsion. Jennie Hatfield-Lyon, the human-rights lawyer from Queen's University who worked with the Toronto firm Davies, Ward and Beck, was also summoned. Bill Spencer, along with daughter Judy, flew in from Moncton; the Lamonts and their supporters arrived from British Columbia. They were given three hours of the committee's time, during which they reviewed why they wanted External Affairs to seek expulsion.

Many parts of their submission were credible and convincing. They questioned the use of torture to discover where Abílio Diniz was being held, legitimately protesting that it was a barbaric act. They also told the committee members that the only reason Christine and David had been spared torture was because their lawyers had been present. But Canadian consul Pierre Pichette remembers a completely different situation and is convinced that São Paulo police were well aware of with whom they were dealing and that there was no such threat to the Canadians.

The Lamonts' Brazilian lawyers mistakenly told the committee that the Canadian official did not go to the police station, even though Pichette had accompanied the prisoners on the bus to the station and remained there for several hours. It was Marilyn who gave the committee Christine and David's reasons for using false passports: "If you enter a country using a false name, a false passport, and you establish your identity under that passport, and then you become aware that you're being followed, there's a death squad on your trail or you're in danger in some way, you get out your real passport and exit the country. This is how it protects you."

The Lamonts also submitted a sworn statement by Professor Ronald Newton, Christine's Latin American history professor at Simon Fraser University, attesting to the fact that he had heard of human-rights workers using false passports to flee dangerous situations. Professor Newton was one of the couple's strongest supporters and aided Christine's family throughout much of their ordeal.

In their presentation to the committee, the Lamont and Spencer supporters seemed to have a good reason for everything. Reporters had noticed on other occasions the ease with which anything incriminating was explained away.

New Brunswick Conservative senator Mabel Margaret DeWare, who joined the committee for the hearings, asked for clarification on the false passports.

"Did they have two sets of passports, Ms. Hatfield-Lyon?"

"Yes, they did," replied Hatfield-Lyon.

"They had their Canadian passports as well as [the false passports]?"

"Yes," said Hatfield-Lyon, who, in presenting the case as it was brought to her by the families, had no way of knowing exactly what Christine and David were doing and what documentation they had with them at any given time.

In fact, Christine and David were not carrying their own Canadian passports at the time of their arrest. Marilyn Lamont's explanation for the couple's having a duplicate set of passports could not have worked for her daughter and her fiancé since they did not have the second set with them but had left them in Nicaragua. They were not being followed by death squads; they had assumed a second identity in order to carry out a crime. All traces of who they really were had been left in another country, thousands of kilometres away.

Four days after the Lamonts and Bill Spencer made their presentations to the committee, Barry Mawhinney, the legal adviser to Barbara McDougall and the man who oversaw the legal report giving the department's reasons for recommending against expulsion, was grilled by the committee members for three hours.

It seemed that all the difficult questions that the committee had failed to ask the Lamonts and Bill Spencer about their children did not mean they were prepared to be equally soft on the department's official.

Mawhinney, a respected, high-ranking career civil servant, had served as Canada's ambassador to Czechoslovakia in the late 1980s and in a variety of other high-profile posts before taking up the stewardship of the legal department at External Affairs. His task before the committee was not an easy one.

Mawhinney did manage to clear up some of the families' charges. They stated, for example, that Judge Barioni had been removed from the bench because his original sentences of eight years for Christine and ten for David were not viewed as severe enough by interfering Brazilian politicians. Mawhinney was able to tell the committee that in fact Barioni had been transferred to a financial court magistrate's position in another district that was closer to his home. He did not, however, counter the impression left with the committee that expulsion was a routine matter in Brazil. The Lamonts' lawyers indicated that the type of expulsion they were asking for happens frequently, when in fact, at the time the committee met, it had never been used to free a convicted criminal unconditionally before sentence had been served.

Mawhinney defended his department's integrity and work, but he could not overcome the basic sympathy MPs of all stripes felt for the Lamonts and Bill Spencer.

"As we all know, in South America primarily, it could be any one of our children," said Blaine Thacker, the Lethbridge MP. NDP MP Ian Waddell from Port Moody–Coquitlam in B.C., echoed Thacker's sentiments.

"Guilty or innocent, they could in fact be misguided people who were taken advantage of by these other people in solidarity for the cause. I come from the left wing, so I know a little bit about this solidarity and how people can be involved. There but for the grace of God goes me in my younger days," said Waddell.

These sentiments prevailed and resulted in a sort of victory for the families in their ongoing battle. The committee unanimously called upon Barbara McDougall to "request without undue delay the expulsion of Christine Lamont and David Spencer in accordance with the laws of Brazil and Canada's international human-rights law obligations." The committee asked the minister to reply within sixty days.

Bob Horner says part of his reasoning in backing the expulsion request was his belief that it was the "mandarins" in Ottawa, the bureaucrats, who were calling the shots, not the minister.

"I didn't buy their story of innocence, but I thought, okay, enough, they've paid the bloody price, let's bring them home," he said.

But Horner did not agree with the Lamonts that Christine and David should be set free upon arrival: "I thought they should be sent home, and the minute they land they should be charged with passport offences and given the criminal record they deserve." But charges against Christine and David in Canada for passport offences were not even a possibility. Canadian law requires what is known as "continuity of evidence" to prosecute a case. Without being able to convince a Canadian court that the stolen passports had been kept secure from the day they were first discovered in the kidnap house on Praca Hachiro Miyazaki in São Paulo to the day they were presented as evidence in a courtroom, no case could be built against the pair. It was a technicality, but an important one.

Ultimately, the committee's work, the time and money that the Lamonts spent on pulling together their elaborate presentation, the cost of flying their lawyers from Brazil to Ottawa — none of it made a difference.

In June 1992, the prime minister attended the Earth Summit in Rio de Janeiro and met with Brazilian president Fernando Collor de Mello. Mulroney refused to reveal exactly what was said during the private discussion with Collor, but he did say that those Canadians who were under the impression that Canada could simply ask for the expulsion of Christine and David and have it granted were sorely mistaken.

"This is not an accurate assumption, and people ought to set it aside," Mulroney said, adding that the president had never before used his power to expel a prisoner. Observers believe Mulroney may have bluntly asked what the outcome of such a request would be and been told that there was no chance two convicted terrorists were going to be allowed to walk free. McDougall's officials had read the signals in Brazil accurately when they had determined that the Lamonts were oversimplifying the idea of expulsion. Mulroney's message to the House of Commons upon his return was that he, like McDougall, was concerned about the sentences, but he backed his minister's decision.

When McDougall did reply to the Justice committee's recommendations, well past the sixty-day deadline, she told the committee that she had not changed her mind. What's more, and what McDougall did not mention to Horner in her letter, is that the issue, despite the publicity, despite David Humphreys's hard work, despite ambushing the prime minister at the fund-raiser, despite everything, never so much as made it to the Cabinet table for discussion.

"It never once came up in Cabinet," said McDougall.

This was not for the Lamonts' lack of trying.

CHAPTER 25

THE CONSPIRACY THEORY

BARBARA MCDOUGALL REMAINED FIRMLY ENSCONCED ATOP THE Lamonts' list of adversaries in their bid to free Christine. It was not by accident that she was constantly portrayed as the only obstacle preventing the correction of a bitter wrong — it was entirely by design.

David Humphreys helped the Lamonts and their supporters to come up with a strategy that would dump all the blame for the government's inaction at the feet of McDougall. Humphreys was clear in telling the Lamonts that the prime minister, despite his own inaction on the case, should not be tainted by their criticisms; after all, he could still overrule McDougall. The strategy was clear — this woman, who had no children of her own, who appeared so at home in a man's world, was to be the fall-guy for all criticism heaped on Ottawa.

Just one month after the Justice committee made its recommendations, Keith charged that McDougall and her department were engaged in a right-wing conspiracy to keep his daughter in prison.

The Lamonts alleged that Christine's and David's families were the subjects of investigations by the Canadian Security Intelligence Service, which was operating clandestinely and had been following Christine and David on their initial travels to Central America.

"We are the victims of a conspiracy by External Affairs to stonewall us at all costs and keep Christine and David imprisoned in Brazil," said a tired, defeated-looking Keith at a Vancouver news conference. He was no longer as quick to smile as he had once been. Reporters who had followed the case could see how he had aged since his daughter's arrest. Keith had stepped down from his position as head of surgery at Langley Memorial Hospital, citing as a reason the fatigue and constant pressure induced by fighting for his daughter. Marilyn bore the dark circles under her eyes of someone who never got a good night's sleep. This was the side of their fight that was not by design, that was simply the tragedy of parents at a loss to fulfil the instinctual calling to help a child in need. They fought on.

In a November 1992 memo from David Humphreys to "Core supporters of the Lamont-Spencer campaign," Humphreys explains the ongoing work on Christine and David's behalf: "We have to grasp every opportunity to keep the case alive and continue to put pressure on the government. The strategy is to focus all criticism on McDougall and External while appealing to the Prime Minister to request the expulsion."

McDougall would come under fire from supporters because she was making a decision on a legal matter without being a lawyer herself, as though her judgment was impeded by having never been called to the bar. Barbara McDougall's long list of qualifications, her expertise in finance mixed with her long stint as a volunteer with the Elizabeth Fry Society, which works with women inmates across Canada, was handily ignored. Someone who didn't know better, taken in by the Humphreys-inspired campaign, would think Barbara McDougall, a former vice-president with the investment firm Dominion Securities Ames Ltd., and former executive director of the Canadian Council of Financial Analysts, had gone from being aproned housewife to being External Affairs minister without learning anything along the way.

David Humphreys's memo goes on to explain the decision to place an advertisement in the nationally distributed *Globe and Mail* on October 27, 1992: "Its purpose is to maintain momentum, achieved following the riots, until after the House of Commons returns on November 16 and other activities can be taken to continue the public pressure on the government."

Deadly riots in adjacent prisons in São Paulo in October 1992 had not touched either Christine's or David's prison but had garnered media attention and generated stories in the press, which quoted the Lamonts as being fearful for their daughter's safety. The immediate danger to Christine's and David's health was now part of the strategy to get them released.

It was George Rideout, Bill Spencer's MP in Moncton, who had risen in the House of Commons the previous spring and announced that, after speaking with Christine's parents, he now understood that she was being placed at great risk of contracting the AIDS virus if she was not "rescued" from her Brazilian prison.

Memos from Humphreys also explain the importance of not making Keith and Marilyn the centre of attention. They were not to be portrayed as the driving force behind the campaign to free their daughter: "It's important that the government and public understand that the families are not campaigning on their own but are backed up by a national committee which has a life of its own." It was David Humphreys, an employee of the Lamonts, who gave this so-called grass-roots committee its name. After publication of the advertisement in *The Globe and Mail*, the committee was to be formally known as Canadians for Justice for Christine Lamont and David Spencer. The phone number and mailing address given out continued to be the Lamonts' basement office in

Langley. In addition to the introduction of the formal committee to the Canadian public, the *Globe* advertisement also took the Lamonts down a dubious path when it asked for donations. This idea, again, came from David Humphreys in a memo to supporters: "Fighting the government is expensive. The families have had to spend an enormous amount in their fight to date. The *Globe* ad alone cost more than $8,000. Solicitation of funds isn't everyone's cup of tea. All of you have already given in time and effort that is deeply appreciated. But if anyone receiving this bulletin has any ideas, or would be willing to do any kind of fund-raisng, we would be most happy to co-operate with help or information."

The last line of the national ad, which ran on page A15, stated: "Donations and letters of support will be gratefully used to assist in a costly campaign against our own government — which uses public money to defend its mistakes."

The pressure was unrelenting. Barbara McDougall described the campaign by the Lamonts and David Humphreys as comparable to "trying to sleep with a mosquito in the room. They were always there, not really doing any harm, but always there."

The timing of *The Globe and Mail* ad was designed to coincide with the national unity referendum that was drawing Canadians to their morning newspapers. Christine's sisters, Elisabeth and Heather, used the opportunity of McDougall's visit to Vancouver to make a speech on behalf of the "Yes" forces supporting the constitutional-unity deal that had become known as the Charlottetown Accord to ambush the minister. McDougall remembers the confrontation as being little more than a show for the cameras.

"All that takes a real strategy on their part," McDougall said, referring to the timing that coincided with the national media's presence at the speech. "That was not an outburst of emotion. Everything became more orchestrated, more manipulative as time went on."

For the Lamonts, of course, it was not manipulation, it was

survival. Christine's life was at stake. No measures were too extreme, no accusations too preposterous.

When the president of Brazil was forced to step down, along with his cabinet, in a corruption scandal in September 1992, the situation seemed even worse, since any contacts they had made in Brazil, any progress made with the Collor government, was now eradicated.

Humphreys faxed copies of letters written by Christine and David from their jail cells, claiming innocence, to newspapers across the country. Some papers published them. Ads were taken out in the community paper in Barbara McDougall's St. Paul's riding in Toronto, telling her constituents that she was unwilling to help their daughter, who "is not that different from your daughters, with her idealistic and noble goals of helping to rid the world of injustice. . . . We are decent Canadians, but when the chips were down, our government refused to help bring justice to our family."

Humphreys, along with much-loved Toronto cartoonist Ben Wicks, visited the editor of the *The Toronto Star*, John Honderich, in the hopes of drumming up support from the nation's largest newspaper. The suggestion was put to Honderich that the *Star* launch a "Free Lamont and Spencer" campaign. Their hopes were dashed when veteran reporter Dale Brazao, who had been dispatched to São Paulo in the days following the arrests and who had followed the case, told the editor that there were too many unanswered questions surrounding the case, and too much evidence pointing to their guilt for the *Star* in good conscience to demand that these "two, young, innocent Canadians" be freed.

Humphreys and the Lamonts organized rallies in Toronto and Ottawa, and arranged for a meet-the-press day with Marilyn in Toronto's elegant Royal York Hotel in February 1993, in the hopes of winning over reporters in eastern Canada, closer to Ottawa's corridors of power.

The religious side of the campaign was still vigorously pursued.

Humphreys drafted a letter to be signed by the leaders of four Christian churches that would then be sent on to the prime minister, asking for a meeting to discuss the case. Unfortunately, Anglican archbishop Edwin Lackey, who was supposed to sign the letter on behalf of the other representatives, died just days before the letter was to be sent in early 1993, putting the plan on hold.

There was talk of asking the Senate Standing Committee on External Affairs to review the case, since the equivalent parliamentary committee continued to refuse to hear them. An interview was booked on CBC's "Morningside" with Peter Gzowski. Every possible angle was being chased, every chance being taken, nearly every penny of the Lamonts' retirement savings being spent.

The Lamonts had travelled to Brazil in December 1992 after a call from the Canadian consulate informed them that Christine had requested a doctor and was suffering from swollen ankles. Keith and Marilyn left the next day. The consulate had arranged for Christine to be examined by a doctor attached to the Canadian government, and blood and urine tests were ordered. This was not enough for the Lamonts. For them, this was the last straw: their daughter was obviously ill and they were convinced that their worst fears had been realized, that Christine had contracted hepatitis or HIV while in prison. Although Christine recovered from her bout with swelling in the joints, the tests discovered that she carried a dormant strain of tuberculosis, to which doctors believe she had been exposed in Canada as a child. She showed no symptoms of the illness developing, but the test results gave her parents one more piece of ammunition to use in demanding her expulsion, saying it was just a matter of time before she developed the respiratory disease.

At her wits end, and with panic rising that her daughter's health was in danger, Marilyn Lamont announced that she and her husband would be suing Barbara McDougall and the federal government for refusing to protect the lives of the jailed Canadians as guaranteed under the Canadian Charter of Rights and Freedoms. An independent report from lawyers in Saskatchewan called the case a good test of whether or not the Charter applied to citizens outside Canada, effectively attempting to transfer Canadian laws to another country. However, the suit was never launched.

An example of the use of the expulsion provision in the Brazilian constitution was uncovered. The Lamonts said that a convicted murderer, a Chilean, had been returned to Chile from Brazil using the expulsion procedure. The expulsion had been signed by Itamar Franco, Brazil's new president, who had taken over after the Collor scandal. They presented this instance as proof that the new regime in Brazil was willing to use that provision of the constitution. It took McDougall's department to point out the differences between the two cases. In a response to a query from Bob Horner, McDougall stated: "Oswaldo Enrique Ramos was living in Brazil under a false name and carrying a false passport. During the period 1973–76 he was associated with the Chilean Security Service and it is alleged that his role was to provide information on individuals who were to be interrogated and to decide which individuals should be executed or otherwise made to disappear. The Chilean authorities wanted him in order to provide information on individuals who disappeared during that period. I understand he is seriously ill with diabetes, and the Chilean authorities were anxious to get his information before he dies. This is clearly not a case of an individual convicted and imprisoned in Brazil."

For McDougall, this was another clear case of the sort of manipulation that had become the stock-in-trade of the Lamonts' strategy to free Christine. The Lamonts themselves brushed off the idea that they had become almost professional publicists. They continued to believe they were winning support that would eventually push Ottawa to act.

Their "one-page summary of the case," released in November 1992, is rife with misleading statements — true to an extent, but taken out of context to suit their purposes. It stated: "The trial judge admitted there is reasonable doubt about their guilt." Judge Barioni maintains to this day that he was completely convinced of their guilt. "The use of torture in the case and the cruel and unusual treatment of the two Canadians have been established." This sentence left readers believing that the pair had been tortured, something that never happened. Details of the most damning evidence, the use of false Canadian passports, is not included in the summary, which was handed out to prospective supporters at rallies and to churchgoers on Sunday mornings.

Through all the campaigning, not once did the name Abílio Diniz ever come up. Not once did the undisputed victim of this crime ever figure into the discussion. The Lamonts maintained that "Abílio Diniz was extremely well treated during that kidnapping." Perhaps they did not know of his ongoing psychological problems, maybe they hadn't seen images of the weakened, drawn-looking man as he emerged from the kidnap house. Oddly enough, the family's words echoed those of the protesters outside the courthouse when the Squamish Five had been tried: no one had been killed; therefore, no real harm had been done.

Abílio had been all but forgotten, relegated to a secondary status as being less important and deserving of people's attention than Christine and David. They had emerged quite clearly as the new, truer victims in this crime. As Canadians, they were somehow more deserving of our sympathy.

Barbara McDougall said she felt David Humphreys urged the Lamonts on in their struggle for Christine, as he searched for new ways to press the government to change its mind. When he met with party workers, he told them he had taken on the case as a favour, that he was doing this work "pro bono" because he honestly believed that the pair were innocent. The Lamonts, however, in detailing their struggle to free their daughter, refer to the cost involved in having a lobbyist and publicist on their side.

Humphreys would later concede that, yes, his firm was billing for its services, but, he would add, it was at a reduced rate because of his belief in their innocence.

Supporters from a local United Church in Ottawa who were among the fifteen people who showed up for that rally on Parliament Hill on February 11, 1993, to hear Marilyn call for her daughter's return to Canada were shocked to learn that the passionate young man leading the group in chants, calling for Canada to "Bring Them Home," was not a friend of Christine and David, but rather an employee of Humphreys, paid to get the crowd going and give them tips on demonstrating on the Hill.

"It was a rude awakening for me," remembers one church member and supporter. "I wasn't under any illusions that they were innocent, but I thought they should be brought home anyway. But this, this paid protester, was too much for me. I vowed to call it quits that freezing cold day."

That same supporter, a long-time human-rights worker in Canada, would later call the entire campaign "an example of middle-class pressure gaining preferential treatment."

Nothing was more damaging to the Lamonts than the suggestion that their obvious prosperousness was buying them access to Ottawa and Brazil's powerhouses. Ordinary people, be they Canadians or Brazilians, are not often granted audiences with senior ministers. The Lamonts say this is irrelevant to their daughter's legal case, and they are right. But it is not irrelevant to their daughter's story. It was the money, and Christine's knowledge that it would always be there, that allowed her to follow the path she chose, that allowed her to put off making life's hard choices, that allowed her the freedom to head to Latin America, knowing that, no matter what happened to her, her parents would be there for her, chequebook in hand.

Keith turns the issue of money around, saying that the family's obvious resources meant that Christine would have no reason to kidnap for ransom, that the money she needed to follow her dreams would be provided by them. But Christine was not looking for tuition money for school, insurance money for her car, or cash for a plane ticket home. She and her colleagues in kidnapping were looking for the millions of dollars needed to sustain an extreme cause, even to fight wars.

The irony of the Lamonts' relative wealth and Christine's actions is that, had she been Brazilian, had her family lived their well-heeled lifestyle in Rio de Janeiro or São Paulo, her father, Keith, or even Christine herself, might well have been the target of kidnappers.

As time passed and McDougall refused to alter her position and adhere to the recommendations of the Justice committee, Keith and Marilyn began to push to have Bob Horner revisit the issue. In a plea for more support, they sum up what they are looking for: "We are still looking to the Justice Committee to help us bring our beloved daughter home. She is not, and has never been, a terrorist and we love her very much."

This one sentence seems to capture everything Keith and Marilyn had been feeling for almost three years. Their Christine, their beloved, at times, misguided daughter, needed them, and they were not prepared to let her down.

CHAPTER 26

BUZON DE SANTA ROSA

CANADA ENTERED A PERIOD OF POLITICAL TURMOIL AT THE START of 1993. Prime Minister Mulroney seemed to be wavering about whether or not he would stay on as Tory leader through one more election. Then, on February 24, he announced his resignation. The race to replace him began. At first the Lamonts panicked as Barbara McDougall's name was tossed out as a possible successor. But, within a matter of weeks, it was clear that the Class of '84, Mulroney's crew of seasoned politicians who had come with him to office almost a decade earlier, would "follow the leader," with many of them bowing out of not only the race for the leadership, but politics as well. Kim Campbell emerged as the candidate most likely to succeed Mulroney, and on March 14, McDougall made it known that she was out of the race and out of Ottawa come June, when the leadership convention was to be held in the nation's capital.

Meanwhile the Lamonts' support group was renamed. It was now known as the Lamont-Spencer Political Action Network

(LSPAN) — punchier, shorter, and stating without pretence that the lobby to free Christine and David had become a political issue that was meant to influence the way people voted in the election that was to be called before the end of the year.

The Lamonts viewed this election as a new opportunity. A government with Kim Campbell, a B.C. native, at the helm, a new External Affairs minister, some pre-election goodwill — it could all culminate in an expulsion request. The Lamonts geared up to make sure delegates at the leadership convention knew that they were not going away. They were set to hand out leaflets at the door, to demand to know where MPs stood on the issue of expulsion, to once again catch the attention of the national media. Liberal leader Jean Chrétien, who had begun his unofficial election campaign with a bus tour of the Maritimes, had stopped in David Spencer's home town of Moncton just long enough to vow to bring the Canadians home if elected. Things were looking up.

The Lamonts' hopes had been raised many times in the previous three and a half years, only to be dashed by an unyielding government. This time felt different. An air of optimism kept them going, kept them dealing with interview requests, churning out press releases, sending messages of love and encouragement to Christine to keep her own hopes up inside her jail cell.

But once again, something would go wrong. This time it had nothing to do with Barbara McDougall, with stubborn bureaucrats, or with Brazilian influence-peddling by interfering politicians. This time the culprit was a spark from a lit cigarette.

Shortly after 1:00 a.m. on May 23, 1993, the best auto-repair shop in Managua, Nicaragua, was blown apart by an explosion heard across the vast, flat city.

The Taller de Santa Rosa was a popular garage, which many foreign diplomats and aid workers relied on for the upkeep of their four-wheel-drive trucks and jeeps that absorbed some of the shocks of pot-holed Managuan streets. The Taller de Santa Rosa was also the property of Miguel Larios Moreno, the Basque separatist who had obtained Nicaraguan citizenship in 1982 and appeared to have turned respectable in Managua's small-business community. The explosion revealed that appearances can be very misleading.

One of the many foreigners who relied on the Taller was a Swiss national who must question to this day just what he did to deserve such bad luck. Not only was his red Volkswagen in for repairs on the night of the blast, and subsequently ended up a blackened shell, but police assumed that he was somehow involved. It was not his car being in the lot that cast suspicion on the Swiss man, but rather the twelve surface-to-air missiles found in the trunk. (He was later released when police realized that his car was being used without his knowledge to transport illegal arms as part of a black-market deal.)

As the flames were doused, police and local military officials who were called to the scene began taking inventory of the array of weaponry lying around. Most of the arms survived the blast completely intact, mainly because of the forethought of the garage's builders, who had used reinforced steel in constructing their underground warehouse and had equipped it with hydraulic doors. Otherwise there would have been nothing left for authorities to examine, and houses would have been levelled for blocks.

Amid the ashes, pyjama-clad former Sandinista leaders, who were now just ordinary citizens after their election defeat in 1990, surveyed the damage. Local residents, who had fled their homes before flames struck, marvelled at the number of former high-level government officials milling around in the predawn haze — Tomás Borge, the former intelligence chief, among them.

During this frenzy of activity, several journalists from the newspaper *La Barricada* managed to sneak away with some of the thousands of pages of documents that were exposed to view when police discovered the hydraulic door to the underground cache. The primary concern of Managuan police and the army on May 23 was not documents, but rather the nineteen missiles, hundreds of Chinese-made AK-47 assault rifles, machine-guns, rocket-propelled grenades, and tons of ammunition and explosives, including C-4, a key ingredient in terrorist bombs. In the immediate aftermath of the explosion, police weren't too concerned about what happened to some scraps of paper floating around.

The weapons were later traced to the Farbundo Martí National Liberation Front, specifically the Popular Liberation Forces, which Christine and David had been associated with during their time in Managua. As part of U.N.–brokered peace accords in El Salvador, the FMLN had vowed that all weapons had been destroyed. The explosion at Santa Rosa was now threatening the first taste of peace the people of Salvador had known in more than a decade.

On the morning after the explosion, the discovery of the weapons cache and its significance would be the news. The front page of *La Barricada* was plastered with news of the "Buzon de Santa Rosa," the two men police suspected were dead, and a third who had been mysteriously dropped off at a local hospital by an unidentified man who then vanished. But what most newspaper readers in Managua stared at as they picked up that same day's edition of the colourful, broadsheet paper, were the six different pictures of Christine Lamont and David Spencer that stared back at them.

Within days, Romeu Tuma, Sr., the former head of the Brazilian federal police who was now that nation's representative with Interpol and the North and South American vice-president of the multinational policing organization, would finally have some hard evidence to substantiate his long-standing theory, which he shared with his son, Romeu, Jr., that Abílio Diniz's kidnapping was the act of an international leftist terrorist ring. Tuma had waited almost four years for his "missing link." Among the wreckage from the garage that he had also been handed was what appeared to be the plans to kidnap three other Brazilians and two Mexicans, all of which had been successfully carried out, with a combined profit to the kidnappers of about U.S.$10 million.

This goldmine of information had been handed to him courtesy of what police speculate was a careless error on the part of the men hired to move the arms, something as stupid as a lit cigarette that set off the explosion.

La Barricada's reporters would later explain that they didn't even know who the Canadians were when they ran their pictures on page one, which is why there is no mention of them in the accompanying story. They simply used pictures selected at random from the cache to give readers an idea of what they had found.

Officials from the local judiciary demanded that the newspaper hand over all the documents it had obtained. Reporters grudgingly obliged and, as near as officials could tell, the stash of documents was once again complete.

When the arms cache had been itemized and counted, authorities realized they had found weapons enough to equip a small army — or a massive terrorist assault. Underworld customers at the Taller de Santa Rosa could also pick up one of more than three hundred foreign passports, drivers' licences, or other identification documents to ensure a clean getaway. Santa Rosa was, in the great American tradition of Woolworth and Kmart, one-stop shopping. Except these shoppers were in the market for the tools of terror.

Authorities moved quickly to find the operator of the garage, but Miguel Larios Moreno was nowhere to be found. After dropping off the injured man at the hospital, he had disappeared. This strikes observers as odd, since Managua is a land-locked city. If Moreno didn't flee by air, which is next to impossible, given security at the airport, then there was ample chance for the borders to be alerted of his approach. The popular theory is that Moreno remained hidden in Nicaragua until a plan could be devised to smuggle him safely out of the country.

In the days after the blast, Sandinista finger-pointing became popular, with different factions claiming that the others had knowledge of the arms business operating in Santa Rosa. One former Sandinista handed the government a list of three ETA Basque separatists living in Managua. President Violeta Chamorro's government arrested and deported the men to Spain, where two of them faced a total of seven charges for murder, including the 1973 assassination of Spain's prime minister. Rival Sandinistas decried the deportations. The government was given the names of four other men, who were subsequently arrested in connection with the arsenal. Everyone involved with the case was certain of one thing: it would have been virtually impossible for the arms business to have operated without the direct knowledge and indirect consent of the Sandinistas while they were in power. And, even more alarming for international observers, the cache could not have continued to operate well into 1993 without the approval of high-ranking military officials in Nicaragua — namely, the Sandinista-controlled military and intelligence departments, which merged after Violeta Chamorro's election victory brought an abrupt and unexpected end to Sandinista rule in 1990.

News of the blast, known as the buzon, and the documents revealed in its aftermath took several weeks to work its way into the international press. One of the reasons for the delay was the initial confusion surrounding the discovery and significance of the papers, which were being amassed in a judge's small office in the local courthouse in Managua. Another reason, no doubt, was that Nicaragua had not been especially newsworthy since the installation of the Chamorro government and the end of the U.S.–backed Contra war against the ruling Sandinistas under Daniel Ortega. The dozens of foreign correspondents who had spent months on end at Managua's Hotel Inter-Continental had gone elsewhere in search of fresh conflict. But with news of the Buzon de Santa Rosa, they would soon be back.

CHAPTER 27

No More Answers

When news filtered back to Canada about the explosion and the subsequent discovery of Canadian documents, it was accompanied by very few details. No one in Ottawa could even confirm that Canadian officials had viewed the documents, apart from the passports.

Reports from foreign media, be they Nicaraguan, American, or Brazilian, gave varying accounts of what was found. The reporter for *The Toronto Star* who had covered the initial arrests in Brazil was in Europe on assignment when the news broke, and I was asked to investigate.

Weeks of research and interviews led only to more confusion, as accounts of what was to be found in Managua varied. The only way to know what was there was for the *Star* to send its own reporter. There were rumours that the judge heading the inquiry into the papers had cut off the access that had initially been granted to a limited number of reporters. The *Star* took the chance, and I was sent to Managua in early July 1993, more than a month after the blast.

The documents were in bulging manila folders, stacked on a long, low table to the right of Judge Martha Quezeda, a justice in Managua's Fifth Criminal Court. She was a Sandinista appointee to the Juzgado Quinto Local de Crimen, but a woman who held the respect of the ruling Chamorro government. Judge Quezeda, unlike so many of her compatriots, is not a warm woman. She is not quick with a smile, but is rather coolly efficient. Quezeda wanted to know whom I represented and why I was interested in the documents. She had had her fill of American media coming into her modest office, expecting a boardroom where they could sift through the papers. She had put the media on notice that she would tolerate very little disruption. She would continue her work hearing pleas and other minor criminal cases while I sat and pored over the papers, which smelled of mould, smoke, and chemicals. She tolerated neither noise nor conversation in her tiny office, with its broken chairs, dirty white walls, flickering fluorescent lights, and tired air conditioner trying its best to cool the stuffy room.

But because I was the first Canadian to see the documents in her possession, Judge Quezeda was interested to know what I could tell her about the various Canadian papers: what they were; how easy they would be to obtain; whether the forgeries were good enough to get by in Canada or had probably been created solely for use in Latin America, where the scrutiny would be less intense. She put up with me in her tiny office for a week, allowing me to rummage through the folders.

The box of personal papers that Christine and David had left behind in Managua when they set out for Brazil had probably been moved to the bunker without their knowledge. The timing of the move most likely coincided with the Sandinista election defeat, which meant that the foreign terrorists, previously tolerated, were forced to go underground.

The amount of information relating to Christine and David was overwhelming at first. In total, there were more than two hundred individual items in the dossiers. Everything was there: plane tickets that made it possible to trace their movements, all their identification in their real names, plus the forgeries they used to make their fake ID that transformed them into Paul Mendes and Lisa Walker. David had practised Mendes's signature over and over again on the back of an old envelope. Blank identification from Simon Fraser's student newspaper was there, along with a press card that had been issued to Rob Taylor, the Salvaide activist whom David and Christine had known in Vancouver. Their letters of reference were all there, including the one supposedly written by Professor Ronald Newton, claiming he had known Christine for seven years. Another letter, by a non-existent professor at Simon Fraser, written on university letterhead, turned out to be a reference for Jose Martinez Ramos, the alias of one of the Basque separatists living in Managua.

The time and effort that had gone into creating all of these documents was obviously considerable. Theirs had not been a last-minute decision to change names and use fake ID, but a long-thought-out plan. Their papers were found alongside the list of potential kidnap victims, Abílio Diniz's name among them. Abílio's daily routine, his financial status, his credit card numbers, his children's names, the details of his exercise routine — it was all there. The list of potential targets mirrored those found in one of the kidnappers' apartments in São Paulo when police searched it after Abílio was released. The style used to make the notes, the categories listed — all were identical, as if the same person had designed the format to be used when targets were being followed and studied.

Christine's and David's passports were there. The one Christine had reported missing turned up beside its replacement. Her American passport was also there. Christine's claim that she kept her own passport with her as well as her false one, to use in case of trouble or threats to her safety, was refuted. Jennie Hatfield-Lyon's submission to the Justice committee that Christine and David had two sets of passports with them in Brazil was found to be a mistake.

They had left all traces of their true identities hidden in Managua, far out of the reach of Brazilian authorities, who, if the kidnapping had not gone so terribly wrong, would have been hunting for a Lisa Walker and a Paul Mendes once the trail had led police to the rented houses.

The find in Managua garnered all sorts of interest. Investigators from the U.S. State Department had arrived to see what was there. The Central Intelligence Agency soon followed. The U.S. Federal Bureau of Investigation, probing the February 26, 1993, terrorist bombing of the World Trade Center in New York that killed five people, soon arrived. One of the men accused of plotting the World Trade Center bombing was found to have five Nicaraguan passports in his possession. A search of Ibraham Elgabrowny's Brooklyn home turned up passports in the name of El Sayyid Nosair, his wife, and three children. Nosair was an Islamic extremist who was serving a prison term for weapons offences after being acquitted of the 1990 murder of Rabbi Meir Kahane in New York. It appeared Nosair's getaway plan, like those of so many terrorists before him, had included a trip to Managua. News of a document find in Managua drew the attention of Spanish investigators hunting for Basques, and, of course, Brazil's Romeu Tuma, "The Sheriff," would soon arrive, first to examine the documents, and then to announce plans to reopen the Diniz investigation in the hopes that somewhere among the six thousand pieces of paper in Judge Quezeda's office lay the names or photographs of the members of the kidnapping gang who remained at large. Tuma wanted the people whom Humberto Paz and his cohorts, including Christine and David, had refused to identify.

The papers, the passports, the files — these were the subject of international interest. But tucked away at the rear of the large manila folder marked "5" was a small batch of papers that held little appeal for either the international or the Nicaraguan authorities. In the grand scope of the investigation, they were insignificant, but for the people fighting to free Christine and David from thousands of kilometres away in Canada, they would prove devastating.

The letters that Christine and David had written in advance had never been mailed, despite the instructions on a Post-It attached to the front of each addressed envelope. The letters had not even been opened. It was Judge Quezeda who gave me permission to be the first to read them. These letters offered a chilling view of the daughter Keith and Marilyn loved so much, of the son that Bill Spencer said he was still proud of to this day. It was easy to see from the letters why Christine's family had remained so devoted. These letters — so loving, so happy, so childish in their declarations of love for her family — portrayed the Christine that they knew. The fact that she had been sufficiently calculating to write them in advance — to invent a beautiful Christmas day, a great Easter weekend, heavy storms, leaky roofs, new books she was reading — suggested that there was a side to their daughter that Keith and Marilyn didn't know. The list that she kept of her lies only served to underline the depth of her calculation.

To someone who had never met either Christine or the Lamonts, the letters were heart-breaking. The invented stories, the feigned interest, the pain that they would later cause — all were affecting. In the end, after her parents' fight on her behalf, after all the money spent, after all the tears shed, what was left was a very sad situation. The letters even revealed that Christine wasn't a vegetarian any more, although her mother had told hundreds of people over the years in her bid to free her that she was.

It would not be a pleasant trip to the Lamont home one week later to show them photographs of these phoney letters, along with Christine's list of lies and the other papers and passports.

In the weeks following the blast in Managua, with few details available in Canada, Keith and Marilyn resorted to what had become second nature to them — they came up with answers for everything, a reasonable explanation that "fair-minded Canadians" would accept. The papers, which the Lamonts understood to be quite innocent in nature, had been "planted" by enemies of Christine and David and were not found among the rubble in Santa Rosa. Marilyn, who had no firsthand knowledge of the steel-reinforced bunker, said she found it "very strange" that passports and papers could survive a blast that levelled nearby homes. She and Keith described the bunker as nothing more than an "old-fashioned repair shop." Keith said the family had hired a free-lance journalist in Managua to look into the matter for them and had been told that the Canadian passports were in pristine condition, while the remaining documents were charred and smoky.

Firsthand knowledge of the documents and the bunker itself that undermined their settled interpretation of events did not change their thinking. Neither did the photographs showing much of the Canadian documents complete with singe marks and burns. "No," they said, this had been a plant by anti-Sandinista forces in Nicaragua. Now the enemy of Christine and David was the government of Nicaragua. In answer to this charge by the Lamonts, Nicaragua's Interior minister, Alfredo Mendietta, shrugged and said: "We have 60 per cent unemployment here. We have people who don't have enough to eat. We have terrorists in our midst dealing in rocket launchers. Do these parents think we have nothing better to do than frame their children for crimes in another country? It's ridiculous."

Maria Cristina Argullo, an aide to Mendietta, pointed out the obvious: "No one wants to believe their child would do this," she said. "But if we believed every mother's opinion of their child then we'd have no criminals in the world, would we?"

Still, the Lamonts insisted that there were reasonable explanations for everything. Other people could have assumed Christine's and David's identities; indeed, stamps in their passports indicate that they had been used long after the Canadians had been jailed. David's passport had been used as recently as January 1991. But nothing could explain the letters, with a return address that was not an apartment but a postal box in a neighbourhood known as Monte Tabor. The mailbox was registered to a Salvadorean, again associated with the Popular Liberation Forces. The home address the man had listed when he registered for the postal box turned out to be a non-existent address on a small street tucked behind the French embassy. No one remembers a young foreign couple living in the area, where most people own their gated homes and rent would be very high.

As Keith and Christine's sisters, Heather and Elisabeth, studied the photographs on the back patio of the family home in Langley on a cool summer evening by the pool, a photographer snapping pictures all the time, Marilyn Lamont stared off into the distance. She did not even read what was in front of her. Instead, she was thinking, desperately searching for a reason, an explanation and an answer to somehow minimize the damage that these letters could cause.

These letters portrayed a daughter who was not what they had been telling the "fair-minded" Canadian public and any politician who would listen for close to four years now. They were the work of a liar, a liar who knew that she needed a good memory, a liar who used cheat notes to keep track of her stories.

Marilyn denied that her daughter had written the letters. But the contents were so obviously personal that even Keith admitted that they were his daughter's doing. A handwriting expert had already been hired by the *Star* to confirm that the person who signed Christine's original passports in Ottawa was the same person who had written the letters. Marilyn then said that, if they were Christine's handiwork, then they had been written to reassure her and her husband that they need not worry about their daughter while she engaged in "dangerous human-rights work."

The Lamonts tried very hard to pre-empt the fire that these

letters were about to set. Christine's mother produced cards that Christine had made from her prison cell, using construction paper and silver sparkles to form the dove that is the symbol of Amnesty International, showing the side of their daughter that they knew so well.

But it was already too late. With her daughter and David refusing to speak to reporters from their São Paulo prisons, *The Toronto Star* ran the story of the documents in Managua, leading with the phoney letters. It began: "This is a story about lies . . ."

The letters, the documents, the forgeries, the multiple pictures with different poses, the missing passports that had been recovered — it was all there to speak for itself. Readers could draw their own conclusions.

For the Canadian public, it was too much to swallow. Supporters, despite some brave faces across Canada, had already accepted too much, had already been willing to ignore too many unanswered questions.

Professor Ronald Newton, who had written a reference for Christine that was handed to Judge Barioni during her trial and who had his name on the letterhead of the support group created by David Humphreys, called Canadians for Justice for Lamont and Spencer, backed off from his sworn statement that he knew of people who had used phoney passports during dangerous human-rights work. Newton offered a clarification to the effect that he had only heard of the practice being used in two or three instances in Guatemala, and then only in cases of extreme emergency. When he was told of the phoney letter of reference for Christine with his name on it found amid the dust in Managua, his response was a stunned, "I'll be damned."

The Senate Foreign Affairs committee backed off plans to hear the Lamonts' case for their daughter. David Humphreys decreased his lobbying efforts in the hope that things would cool down before the anticipated fall election. Barbara McDougall, her position now publicly vindicated, expressed sympathy for the parents.

RCMP investigators in Canada, who had never said a word publicly about the case, expressed quiet relief that finally the media had questioned Christine's and David's claims of innocence. They had followed the case closely and knew there was more to it than met the eye. They knew of the duplicate passports. They knew there was no debt that David was running from. They knew of Christine's, and especially David's anarchist and far-left associations when the pair were in Vancouver. They knew of the connection to Chilean Sergio Urtubia. They also knew that the family's public challenge to Canadian authorities that, if they were concerned about the duplicate passports, they should charge Christine and David in Canada, was not realistic. Without continuity of evidence — meaning proof that the passports had been secure since the day in 1989 on which they had been found in the kidnap house — the RCMP could not build a viable case, especially since they had reports that those same passports had somehow been sold on the black market and used to enter and exit Venezuela in the summer of 1992. The police knew all this, but they were glad that someone had finally made it public.

"It's crazy; they had the entire Fraser Valley rallying around them, insisting they were innocent," remembered one veteran investigator, who cynically stated that, through it all, "the only time Lamont and Spencer [Christine and David] tell a lie is when they move their lips."

Sympathy, it seemed, was not as widespread as the Lamonts had thought.

CHAPTER 28

FALLOUT

IN BRAZIL, SYMPATHY FOR THE LAMONTS WAS NON-EXISTENT. Their campaign had not gone unnoticed; in fact, it was closely monitored. The constant criticism, the never-ending pressure for better cells, better meals, more medical care — every possible demand was made of the consulate, whose representatives in turn visited the prison wardens. Despite their greatest efforts to be polite, respectful, and, above all, diplomatic in making their requests that Christine and David not be treated by the prison doctors or dentists, the gist of every request was criticism — and each and every instance could be traced back to the Lamont home. Even Barbara McDougall, with her experience working with female convicts as part of her volunteer activities with the Elizabeth Fry Society, knew that special treatment breeds resentment among other prisoners and can end up making conditions worse in a prison.

"It could in fact be dangerous if they were seen as getting preferential treatment," McDougall said. "The Lamonts couldn't see that."

Consulate staff worked hard to give the wardens the impression that this type of interest was paid to all Canadians in jail abroad. Of course, it's extremely unlikely that any Canadian prisoner has ever received the time and attention lavished on Christine and David. Even those facing the death penalty or life imprisonment for relatively minor drug crimes committed abroad get significantly less notice.

The feeling that the Lamonts' efforts might actually have made matters worse for their daughter was mentioned by *Vancouver Sun* columnist Trevor Lautens not long after the extended sentences were handed down. Sheltered by their friends and supporters, firmly believing that the vast majority of Canadians were in their camp, the Lamonts rarely encountered the opposing view. Lautens barged into their home and straight to their breakfast table with it, along with the morning paper. He called the supporters of Christine and David "morally arrogant" and suggested that their vocal criticism of Brazil's justice system might have actually contributed to the increased sentences. Lautens suggested that perhaps the Canadian government was refusing to request the pair's expulsion because it felt justice had been done.

"Canada should not waste its prestige or diminish its goodwill with Brazil" if the pair are guilty, Lautens wrote.

But by June 1993, when Romeu Tuma announced amid much fanfare that there was more work to be done, more terrorists to be found in connection with the Abílio Diniz kidnapping, Canada's good name within many government offices in Brazil was already a little tarnished.

The people who run Brazil, the people firmly ensconced in its First World, did not find that the reiterated criticisms helped their struggle to build a whole First World nation. They didn't need Canada looking down on them with a "holier than thou" attitude. Similarly, the average Brazilian remembered well the act of terrorism inflicted upon one of its favourite sons, and they remembered the Canadians who were involved. The blast in Managua once again sent the Abílio Diniz kidnapping right back to where it had been three and a half years earlier — on the front page of every newspaper and as the lead item every night on the newscasts. Anyone who had forgotten the Canadian involvement was reminded of it by the Brazilian media. The press would not tire of the story of the Canadians, and the timing was, once again, dreadful for those hoping for their release.

The much-touted and long-delayed Transfer of Offenders Treaty, which could bring Christine and David home to serve their jail time in Canada and make them eligible for parole, had been ratified in Ottawa more than a year earlier. In the summer of 1993, as the investigation into their involvement with international terrorists was growing daily, the treaty finally slipped through Brazil's Chamber of Deputies, or lower house, on June 2 and made its way to the Brazilian Senate for ratification. It would then be signed by President Itamar Franco. Canadian diplomats had been driven in their work to get the treaty through. Canadian ambassador William Dymond had paid visits to politicians to ensure the treaty's safe passage through political channels. With Brazil's elected officials' preoccupation with the growing mountain of domestic issues at any one time, the treaty had taken a backseat.

The Lamonts had never expressed any interest in using the treaty to bring Christine and David home, saying that innocent people should not be stuck with criminal records and jail terms when they returned to Canada. Even when things looked bleak and the treaty seemed to be their only chance, they chastised Canadian diplomats for lobbying for its ratification, saying they were sending the wrong signals to Brazil, possibly jeopardizing an expulsion request, should one ever come from Ottawa.

As the fall-out of the blast in Managua, the "Buzon de Santa Rosa," grew with each passing week, it became more and more difficult for the Lamonts to counter every allegation against their daughter and her fiancé. Lawyers were sent to the prison to get sworn statements from Christine and David saying they had no connection to any of the documents found in Brazil. They stated that anything bearing their real, or assumed, names had been forged without their knowledge. They said their phoney letters were written to alleviate worry, but when they realized how impractical the plan was, they had abandoned it. They did not say why the letters were not simply torn up and thrown away. They did not explain how it came about that the handwriting on so many of the forged documents was indistinguishable from their own. Nor did they have an explanation for the dozens of passport pictures they had had taken in such a hurry. Finally, they didn't explain why, if they had obtained two sets of passports to enable them to escape a dangerous situation, they had left one set behind in Nicaragua. The Lamonts fired off press releases condemning *The Toronto Star* for printing the details of the Managua blast without interviewing Christine and David, but Christine and David had refused to be interviewed. Their press releases quoted a law professor from Cambridge University saying the stories should be illegal, and lawyers in Vancouver saying they should sue for libel.

A press council complaint alleging irresponsible journalism by *The Toronto Star* would later be launched and subsequently dismissed. When it all came to an end, *The Toronto Star* had decided to print a story that was backed by the only possible defence — truth.

This time, all of the Lamonts' damage control had very little effect on the blood-letting of their support in Canada. It was too late; the misleading information had been too much for too long. The calls and letters of support from Canadians coast to coast, some twenty thousand of whom had signed petitions demanding their release, dried up. The Lamonts retreated into silence for the first time in years, and waited for the federal election vote in October 1993.

With letters of assurance from Opposition leader Jean Chrétien and other high-profile Liberals, the massive Liberal majority brought in on October 25 might have seemed an answer to their prayers. Lloyd Axworthy had been External Affairs critic in the Liberal Opposition for years and was widely expected to take up the ministerial mantle when Chrétien announced his Cabinet. The Lamonts told friends privately that they expected their daughter home by Christmas.

But it was veteran politician André Ouellet who was given the plum job at External, now called Foreign Affairs. And just two weeks after being sworn into Cabinet, he announced that, as far as he could see, Canada should follow the path set out by his predecessors and continue to push Brazil to sign its half of the Transfer of Offenders Treaty. Barbara McDougall later guessed that Ouellet had been given his first complete briefing on the case and had drawn the obvious conclusions, the same ones that she had drawn three years earlier.

The treaty, despite passing the Senate in Brazil, had been sidelined by scandal in late September. When news broke of Canadian diplomats paying visits to legislators to push for the treaty to be signed and to senior Justice department officials and judges to try to speed along the tiresome appeal of the lengthy sentences, the Brazilian press responded with a vicious backlash that sent senators backpedalling on their support of the treaty. The head of the Senate, Humberto Lucena, was forced to go before a national television audience to deny that the lobbying had taken place. Lucena's speech left him red-faced when it was discovered that part of the text had been pulled straight from a Canadian embassy briefing note on the affair. Other senators who had voted in favour of the treaty began to call for the president to refuse to sign it. Weeks later, Christine's and David's appeal of their twenty-eight-year sentences was denied.

The Lamonts were visibly shaken by Ouellet's announced intentions to push for a treaty and not request expulsion. Marilyn told reporters she was certain there had been a mistake, a misunderstanding, that they had good friends in the Liberal caucus and were certain the decision would be reversed. But the Lamonts did not have friends in Ottawa in any real sense. As many seasoned politicians know, there are very few true friends in Ottawa. There are people who use other people as pawns in a political game, people who benefited from the publicity that the Lamonts were paying so much money and devoting so much time to generate. Svend Robinson continued to rally on their behalf, and their newly elected Reform Party MP, Randy White, despite his own party's firm law-and-order platform and complete intolerance of the very type of violent crime that Christine and David had been convicted of, jumped on the bandwagon. Both politicians were operating from the safe and ultimately powerless Opposition side of the House of Commons.

Even if the Liberals had elected to follow a different path and request Christine and David's return to Canada, the mood in Brazil had changed. The law-and-order hardliners were once again riding a wave of public approval. The ruling class in Brazil continued to feel as though they were prey for kidnappers, and the discovery of some of their names on a list in Managua, accompanied by details of their personal lives, did nothing to ease their minds.

The Lamonts and Bill Spencer went back to David Humphreys, asking him to secure a meeting with Ouellet so they could state, once again, their case on behalf of their children. Ouellet obliged, and the families met with the minister in the early months of the new government. A news blackout has been in effect ever since. Insiders in Ottawa say Ouellet told the Lamonts outright that, if they expected his help in any way, then their intense media campaign, their war of words in the press, and their bickering with reporters and bureaucrats had to stop. The accusations could no longer fly, and the entire situation had to be given time to cool down if Brazil was ever going to be prepared to act again. The treaty remained stalled, and the Brazilian presidential election was less than a year away. Ottawa concluded that the government in Brazil was not about to risk political suicide by releasing the jailed Canadians before an election, which effectively ruled out an expulsion request. If all news of the two disappeared, perhaps the treaty could be signed quietly and the pair returned to Canada. The Workers' Party, which had been tainted by the kidnapping and siege four years earlier, remained distant from the case, fearing the political fall-out could cost them the presidency for a second time. The ruling right wing would not risk sending the wrong signals to the middle and upper classes, the people most likely to become kidnappers' targets.

By now Keith and Marilyn were willing to accept the treaty to get Christine home. The battle had been too long. For the moral victory of bringing their daughter home a free woman, the Lamonts had risked not getting her back at all. If it hadn't been for their constant pressure, Canadian ambassador William Dymond would not have found himself in the offices of judges and Justice department officials. If the quiet pursuit of the Transfer of Offenders Treaty had been allowed to proceed, if the constant criticism of both the Canadian and the Brazilian government had let up for a while, and the people who are paid to be diplomatic allowed to do their jobs, perhaps President Itamar Franco would have signed the treaty without a second thought, and perhaps Christine and David would be back in Canada today, albeit in prison, but a prison close to home, a prison that would include day passes and regular visits with family. Perhaps prison in Canada would not seem so bad after all.

CHAPTER 29

LIFE GOES ON

THROUGH ALL THIS, CHRISTINE AND DAVID HAVE REMAINED IN their respective prisons in the sprawling Carandiru complex in São Paulo, the largest prison in Latin America — model prisoners, both of them.

They have devised a hand signal for the rare times when they catch glimpses of each other through fences or a distant window. They signal a simple "I love you" and continue on. They write letters to each other in Portuguese, which both have learned to speak. On special occasions, such as birthdays, they are allowed to write to each other in English. David, in the company of his fellow kidnappers, still maintains the political convictions that brought him to Brazil in the first place. He is in contact with fellow political idealists, including the ever-likeable Humberto Paz, who knitted a baby blanket for Christine's sister Heather from his own prison cell after he learned she was expecting her first child in the spring of 1993. He is a man who Keith Lamont describes as "a gentle giant–type person." The Lamonts, who might well have been expected to despise Paz, considering what he had dragged their daughter into, have ended up liking him despite themselves. They have been won over by him, much as their daughter and David were years earlier. Judge Barioni's observations about Paz's powers of persuasion proved accurate.

David is still wiry, youthful, and neat. He retains his cynical sense of humour and calm, controlled temperament. Consulate officials who have visited them regularly have noticed that the past year or so has taken a greater toll on Christine. She does not possess David's intense political convictions. She is neither as driven nor as sure of what she preaches. She does not have the same ideological crutches to rely on when times are rough and lonely. She works in a sewing factory in the prison and teaches English to her fellow inmates. She also reached back to her high-school drama courses and her sister Elisabeth's inspiration and started a theatre group that puts on plays for the others. She makes decorative cut-and-paste cards for family and friends. She continues to have her own cell, and is by all accounts a quiet prisoner who reads a great deal.

Perhaps Christine has had a chance to reread Dostoyevsky's *Crime and Punishment*, the book that she told her family in one of her phoney letters home she had stumbled across in Managua. Perhaps she now realizes what the author went to such pains to communicate: that ideology, no matter how noble the intent, cannot be used to justify a heinous crime. In the Russian classic, the crime was the brutal murder of an elderly pawnbroker, a woman who profited from the misfortunes of others, a woman whom the killer decides does not deserve to live. Christine and David, along with the other kidnappers, decided that Abílio Diniz did not deserve his wealth or his freedom. They were prepared even to end his life, and might have done so had police not discovered his location in time to negotiate his release.

David, like Christine, is a model prisoner. He has been given a job in the prison as a janitor. It's a coveted position because it means he is allowed a certain amount of time outside of his cell and helps to keep both his mind and body occupied. His father jokes that, when you are a senior citizen, other older people constantly ask what your children do for a living. "I tell them my son works for the government of Brazil — he's a janitor for them, after all," says Bill Spencer with a sad smile.

David takes correspondence courses in journalism and writes and reads a lot, particularly left-wing newspapers. He is getting by. But Christine, who devoted so much of her energy to loving David, hasn't actually seen him up close since 1990. This must be hard for the woman who drew five little hearts beside his name in her address book. Politics were David's reason for being, but he was Christine's reason.

Both chain-smoke for lack of anything better to do. Christine's teeth, which were always stained, even in Canada, are in worse shape than ever from the tobacco. Their families, concerned for their future health, send them low-tar cigarettes with every visitor. For breakfast, each is given strong Brazilian coffee and bread; lunch and dinner consist of a variety of bean and rice dishes, with very little meat. Despite the monotony, David tells visitors that he is well fed and has no complaints about the food.

Talk of marriage and babies in the future, after their release, has slowed, as if the possibility of returning to a normal lifestyle has been diminished with time spent in the surreal world of a Brazilian jail. On the fifth anniversary of their prison terms, in December 1994, Christine will be thirty-five years old, David thirty-one. The occasion will once again be marked by a vigil in Langley. In Moncton, the anniversary has never been observed. The town David left so many years ago remains the same: marches in the streets simply do not happen.

The Lamonts are, in so many ways, right: Christine and David have paid a heavy price for their crimes. Five years of their lives have passed, wasted, and for nothing. These have been years during which their contemporaries have been building careers and having families. Lisa Walker's young family is growing up. Paul Mendes is on his way to a successful legal career, although he still feels some bitterness towards Christine because of the suspicion she cast upon him. He wonders what would happen if he ever applied to work in litigation for the federal government, knowing that there is a national security file on him sitting in an office of the Canadian Security Intelligence Service, Canada's spy-catchers — thanks to Christine.

There is no doubt that the mood in Brazil at the time of the crime affected the sentence that was passed on the two Canadians. But Canadian judges, like their Brazilian counterparts, reserve the right to consider general deterrence when they hand down a sentence.

The new right-of-centre government in Brazil, led by Fernando Henrique Cardoso may mean a change of heart with regard to the Transfer of Offenders Treaty. It may be quietly signed one day without any fanfare, returning Christine and David to a Canadian jail and, most likely, immediate parole, although parole in Canada is usually granted only after a show of remorse on the part of the accused. Christine and David, after all this time, have yet to express any regret about what happened to Abílio Diniz, because doing so would constitute an admission of guilt. Ultimately, remorse might have made them look human, caring, and deserving of the sympathies of Canadians. It is also possible that the day will come when the government in Brazil puts them on a plane and sends them home to their families, without so much as an explanation.

Either way, few observers believe they will serve their full, harsh sentences in Brazil.

When they do come home, there will be rebuilding to be done. Keith has delayed retirement to pay for his daughter's fight. Marilyn's entire existence has been consumed by her. Bill Spencer wants a chance to get to know his only son, who was a mere boy when he left home and who has turned into a man in one of the worst possible places.

The Diniz family has already begun to rebuild, to shake off the panic, for example, when someone is late for an appointment. They try to let go of the gripping fear, the constant paranoia, that isn't really paranoia at all, but rather a realistic appraisal of life in Brazil. The possibility exists that any one of them could be next, that they are still being watched, their movements recorded for use on another bright morning when they too could be snatched from the street.

However you look at it, all three families have been irreparably damaged. For two of them, the daily fight goes on.

Bill Spencer is a man who does not know what is true about his son and what isn't. He bluntly says that he is the wrong person to ask about David's guilt or innocence, because he is, after all, the parent. Still, he asks that the country he served in war repay him now by helping him gain his youngest child's freedom. It is a simple and heart-wrenching request.

Marilyn Lamont, at least in public, has never come close to such an acceptance and her denial of the evidence has been her burden, heavier for her, perhaps, than for anyone else, even Keith. She is the mother who cannot accept that her child might have committed a terrible crime. Marilyn's steadfast insistence on Christine's innocence may even make it harder for her daughter to come to terms with her own actions when the day comes, the prison doors open, and Christine and David walk free.

INDEX